MATTERS OF STATE

Matters of State

A Political Excursion

PHILIP HAMBURGER

COUNTERPOINT
WASHINGTON, D.C.

LIBRARY OF CONGRESS CATALOGING-IN-PUBLICATION DATA
Hamburger, Philip.
    Matters of state : a political excursion / Philip Hamburger.
      p. cm.
    ISBN 1-58243-084-5 (alk. paper)
     1. United States—Politics and government—20th century. 2. Politicians—United States—History—20th century. 3. Presidents—United States—History—20th century. 4. Presidents—United States—Inauguration. 5. Political culture—United States—History—20th century. 6. Hamburger, Philip—Political and social views. I. Title.
    E743.H235 2000
    973.9—dc21   00–055518

Jacket and text design by Amy Evans McClure
Printed in the United States of America on acid-free paper that meets the American National Standards Institute Z39–48 Standard.

COUNTERPOINT
P.O. Box 65793
Washington, D.C. 20035–5793

Counterpoint is a member of the Perseus Books Group

10 9 8 7 6 5 4 3 2 1

To Nicholas & Sylvan

The future

Are you lost daddy I arsked tenderly.
Shut up he explained.

RING LARDNER
The Young Immigrunts

CONTENTS

ACKNOWLEDGMENTS

S O MANY PEOPLE TO THANK, but special thanks to Pamela
McCarthy, Erin Overbey, Peter Canby, Alice Mulconry, Bruce
Diones, and David Remnick at *The New Yorker;* to Jack Shoemaker,
Trish Hoard, and Heather McLeod at Counterpoint; to inimitable
Mimi Bowling at the Manuscripts and Archives Division of The New
York Public Library; to Peter Matson; to Edith Iglauer Daly; to Bobbie
Bristol (a miracle of editorial judgment); and to Anna Walling
Hamburger——Annabella.

FOREWORD

I AM NOT NOW AND NEVER HAVE BEEN a pundit. But I have been around a long time, seen many large public events, talked with any number of public figures, and have a special fondness for the pageantry and significance of Presidential Inaugurations. I have been to so many of these that I get mixed up reaching an exact count (fourteen, I think?). For this book, I have gathered together pieces dealing with public matters. What follows are the observations of one man who has tried to keep his eyes and mind open. I have never forgotten some words said to me years ago by Harold Ross, the wondrous first editor of *The New Yorker*. We were correcting proofs in his office one evening when he suddenly looked up and said, "Never go cosmic on me, Hamburger." The admonition has been invaluable, especially for diminishing self-importance. Nonetheless, I have certain fundamental convictions: I loathe communism and fascism. The United States Constitution is the greatest political document ever written, with special emphasis on the Bill of Rights. I believe in the separation of church

and state, universal health care, environmental protection, a capital-
ism of social responsibility, drastic campaign finance reform, the right
of a woman to control her body, racial justice, and the inviolable right
to privacy. In some quarters, such thoughts are labeled "liberal" or
"left-leaning." To me, they have nothing to do with labels or directions (Turn right! Turn left!) but simply with common sense, decency,
and the better angels of our nature.

PROLOGUE:
RANDOM NOTES ON
WASHINGTON, D.C.

I FIRST SAW WASHINGTON when I was about ten or eleven, sometime in the mid-twenties. Throughout the land there was a sense of
never-ending prosperity. My father had long promised me a trip to the
nation's capital, and one fine day down we went from New York, by
train. My father was a proud Baltimorean ("People make fun of the
row houses and white marble stoops, but they are spotless and beautiful," he would say), a proud Democrat, and a passionate believer in
social progress. The only quarrel I ever had with this good man was
his fervent defense of President Roosevelt's plan to pack the Supreme
Court. I dissented, considering it a dangerous, impatient assault on
the Court. But I digress. I still vividly recall my sense of wonderment
when I first caught sight of the spatial grandeur of Union Station, at

the broad boulevards and graceful traffic circles. I felt that I was in a sleepy Southern city, an unhurried and comfortable place. My father hired a car and driver who drove us from one end of the place to the other—past the unforgettable and haunting Lincoln Memorial, past the White House (at that time the incumbent was the man H. L. Mencken always referred to as Dr. Coolidge; he was probably napping, but did wake up from time to time to presciently remark that "the business of America is business"), past the myriad embassies, the imposing Capitol and the tree-lined streets. We were sightseers, eager ones, and as we drove from place to place, and stopped to talk with various guards, there was a distinct, healthy, and pleasant sense of courtesy and dignity. The outward manifestations of government seemed vibrant and admirable.

Skip some years. It is 1935, the depth of the Depression, I am twenty-one and have just graduated from Johns Hopkins University. I need a job. So does my father. The mystical ship he has relied upon all his life, the one that is "just about to come in" has sunk, a chimeric vessel lying somewhere in the briny deep. Stroke of luck! Thanks to the father of a classmate I am offered a temporary job in the press department of the newly established Social Security Administration, headed by John Winant, former Governor of New Hampshire. Here was a golden opportunity to become a tiny cog in a vast, innovative life-saving government adventure. In a stroke of political genius, Roosevelt had picked Winant, a Republican, to demonstrate the bipartisan nature of this desperately needed program at aiding the elderly, the sick, the disabled, both the haves and the have nots. Social Security began to work, and has worked, miraculously, to this day, bringing hope to millions. My job was a simple one: I rose at the crack of dawn, left a stifling rented room (no air-conditioning in those days in a tropical city), proudly walked past the White House, arrived at the Social Security office and pored over tens of newspapers from all parts of the country. My job was to summarize any item that mentioned Social Security and place the entire compilation on Governor Winant's desk by 9 A.M. The adage that history repeats itself is all too true: The same sorts of things were being said in 1935 about Social Security that are being said today. For one thing, it was "socialistic."

Americans, said the critics, were a hardy breed, fully capable of handling their own money. (The fact that practically everybody was stony broke did not appear important.) Clipping after clipping spoke of the administration's intention to tattoo numbers on the hands of each Social Security recipient. Most poignant of all were items claiming that the government intended permanently to place the number of each newborn babe on the baby's tender backside. Ludicrous? Lest we forget, Nazis methodically and heinously stamped numbers on the limbs of their concentration camp victims.

The Social Security job ended in about a year, and I felt no deep sense of loss. Government interested me, but work in a bureaucracy did not. I had set my sights on becoming a writer, starting out as a newspaperman, and went back up to New York. I haunted every paper in town. No luck. No luck anywhere. The Depression was still in full force. I landed a job as a sort of secretary-gofer with a remarkable man, J. M. Kaplan, a businessman of great wealth and many philanthropies. He was one of the most complex and fascinating people I have ever known, but I could not then and cannot now delineate exactly what I did for him. He was kind, generous, and a lifesaver. He was paternalistic: Fridays we received free haircuts and lunch at a fancy French restaurant across from our offices on lower Fifth Avenue. One of his many properties was Welch's grape juice, and each Friday the small force in his office (a secretary, an accountant, a fancy lawyer, and myself) received a case of grape juice. Since I lived on the Upper West Side the trip from office to home, with a carton of grape juice, required a cab. The Friday journey pretty much wiped out my week's mighty stipend. But the business of business was not my forte and, still applying on a persistent basis for newspaper work (without success), I received a partial scholarship to the Graduate School of Journalism at Columbia. Mr. Kaplan applauded the move, and up I went to Morningside Heights. The year was a stimulating one, and marked a critical turning point. Thanks to Henry F. Pringle, a professor at the school, a celebrated historian who had won the Pulitzer Prize for his biography of Theodore Roosevelt, and who had been one of *The New Yorker*'s first Profile writers, I received a recommendation to St. Clair McKelway, then the brilliant managing editor of *The*

New Yorker. McKelway hired me in 1939, and Washington seemed far away. So did grape juice. But war was approaching. I had been excluded from the draft (4-F) because of bad eyesight. I was thrilled one day late in 1941 to receive a call from Archibald MacLeish, then Librarian of Congress. Could I meet with him in his office on Saturday afternoon, December 6? Yes, sir, I most certainly could. I met this elegant and articulate man in his bijou office in the Library at the appointed hour. He said that President Roosevelt was anxious to form a group of writers who could explain to the public why so much money was being spent on defense. Could I get a leave of absence from Mr. Ross, perhaps in February, and come down to Washington? I jumped at the idea. The following day was of course Sunday. But it was Sunday, December 7, 1941, "a day that will live in infamy," and America was at war. The next day I went in to say goodbye to Mr. Ross, who rose from behind his desk with a look both of sadness and encouragement, gave me a warm embrace, accompanied by his signature send-off "God Bless."

The Washington work was fascinating, my colleagues a most extraordinary group including Arthur Schlesinger, Jr., McGeorge Bundy, Milton MacKaye, Barbara Wendell Kerr, Kate Douglas, Robert Kintner, and, in beneficent charge of the writers, my mentor, Henry Pringle. Wartime Washington was a dedicated place. We worked long hours. We felt, (I always felt), a sense of guilt at performing desk work while others were fighting. My task was the writing of pamphlets published by the government and distributed in millions of copies throughout the country. One of these, *Divide and Conquer*, outlined in great detail Nazi propaganda methods: the spreading of lies from one end of the earth to the other. The pamphlet was well received and reprinted in hundreds of newspapers throughout the country. The staid *Saturday Evening Post*, which had never reprinted anything before in its long history, printed every word I had written. I did not consider it appropriate in wartime to sign the piece. Somehow it came to the attention of President Roosevelt who asked MacLeish who had written it. To my utter amazement and stupefaction the President phoned me one day at the office to tell me how pleased he was with *Divide and Conquer*. The brief talk with him is, of course, a highlight of my life. MacLeish was succeeded by the learned, impressive Elmer Davis; the original Office of Facts and Figures became the Office of War Information; there was bureaucratic infighting; and I found myself back at *The New Yorker*.

Hold on! The wide-eyed sightseeing boy is now a man in his mid-eighties. He still goes to Washington from time to time (always by train), still loves the pomp and circumstance of an Inauguration, still treasures the peaceful transfer of power. He knows that the sleepy Southern city of his youth is now a metropolis of almost unimaginable world power. But something happens as that train slows down in the approach to Union Station. He can't help himself. He rushes to the right side of the car to catch a glimpse of the white dome of the Capitol and the tip of the Washington Monument. He knows there is a feeling of meanness that he had not felt before. But he cannot wait to walk past the White House, shed a tear at the Vietnam Wall, and pay his respects to the Lincoln Memorial.

May 2000

MATTERS OF STATE

CHAPTER 1

THE GREAT JUDGE

The bedrock of our liberties lies, I feel, in the independence of the Federal judiciary. Absent that, all is lost. And a bedrock was Learned Hand, the legendary judge who presided over the United States Court of Appeals, Second Circuit. I knew of his monumental defense of freedom of speech and the First Amendment, but little more, until Sunday afternoon, May 21, 1944. I was at home listening to a radio broadcast from Central Park. One hundred and fifty thousand new citizens were to be sworn in by Judge Hand, before a million and a half people—the largest crowed ever gathered in the park. We were in the midst of a shattering war, but the tide had turned and D day was just a few weeks ahead. Shortly after 4 P.M. he began to speak on "The Spirit of Liberty." I was transfixed. The words had such clarity, beauty and meaning that I had the curious sensation that I was at Gettysburg, listening to Lincoln. And, like Lincoln, he spoke briefly, barely more than five hundred words. The next morning not a newspaper in town printed a word of the speech. I called the judge in his chambers and said I would like a copy. He seemed pleased. "You *heard* it?" he said. "Come on down." Down I went. We had a long talk and I wrote a piece for Talk of the Town, quoting from the speech. An avalanche of attention followed, and the speech has gone into the canon of great American utterances. The judge and I became friendly. I went to dinner at his home, he came to mine. The moments with him are among the most important of my life. This piece was written for *Life* a few years after our first meeting.

JURISTS ARE BY NATURE ARGUMENTATIVE, and nothing delights them more than to consider the qualities that constitute lasting greatness on the bench. Is the important factor the literary style and grandeur of a judge's opinions? Zeal for uniting the law with the economic realities of life? Sturdy defense of the *status quo*?

Debates of this nature frequently end in an atmosphere of mellow agreement at the mention of Learned Hand, senior judge of the United States Circuit Court of Appeals for the Second Circuit (New York, Connecticut, and Vermont), a robust, stocky man with thick eyebrows and a voice like the crackle of lightning. An impressive number of judges and lawyers consider him the outstanding member of the federal judiciary, the spiritual heir of such judicial giants as Marshall, Holmes, Brandeis, and Cardozo.

Judge Hand was seventy-five in January 1947, and many of his colleagues and friends, more than anxious to pay him tribute, planned testimonial dinners and the presentation of a bust. Typically the Judge tried to keep one step ahead of them in an attempt to scotch their plans. It is his modest and reasoned decision that public tributes have small place in the life of a judge. Nonetheless he could not stop thousands of lawyers and judges the world over from turning their thoughts in his direction, re-examining his opinions and papers and evaluating his lifework. "Learned Hand is the most distinguished living English-speaking jurist," a Supreme Court justice has remarked with deep feeling. Those who insist that a judge must write with the pen of a master will accept no substitute for his prose. "There is a lovely tune in his head," said one of his colleagues on the bench, "and somehow he translates it into words."

To Judge Hand each individual is sacred and entitled to his day in court. His roots are embedded in the deepest and healthiest soil of

American democracy. To discover the essence of that soil he has devoted a lifetime of inquiry, both on and off the bench. "The only America you can love," he once wrote, "is one whose citizens have learned the self-discipline of compliance in the face of truth; the only country which any man has a right to love is one where there is a balanced judgment, justice founded on wisdom, a free spirit and a temperate mind." He conceives of the law as a living organism and of interpretation as an imaginative exercise. Statutes are the result of legislative compromise, he holds, and judges must therefore discover what the authors had in mind while framing them.

Broad generalizations leave him in a cold intellectual fury. Lawyers who attempt to impress him by reminding the court of "those eternal principles of justice ringing down the ages" do so only once. His broad jaw drops in anguish. His bushy gray eyebrows rise in horror. His face, a moment ago as serene and inquiring as Cardozo's, becomes as fierce as Daniel Webster's at the height of a peroration. The courtroom echoes with a sharp crack as he slaps a hand to his brow and leans far back in a tall leather armchair. "Rubbish!" he shouts, almost disappearing from view behind the bench.

The casual observer, watching Judge Hand charge up the front steps of the federal courthouse in New York or preside on the bench with majestic authority, would conclude that he was a tower of self-assurance. Actually he is torn by doubts and constantly re-examines his first principles. "What are the values? Do you know? Believe me, I do not," he will suddenly say to his law clerk during the discussion of a case. Although convinced that permanent solutions to the problems of life do not exist, he belies the thought by a ceaseless pursuit of solutions. "Shakespeare had Learned in mind when he wrote *Hamlet*," a distinguished corporation lawyer said recently. "Twenty-four hours a day he is a thinking being."

His moods are unpredictable. Some months ago he stepped into an elevator at the courthouse deep in thought and with a dejected expression. "Pardon me, Judge Hand," said a stranger, as the elevator started up, "but I thought your opinion yesterday was wonderful." Judge Hand beamed. "Thank you, sir, thank you very much indeed," he said, stepping off at the twenty-fourth floor. Humming, he walked briskly through his suite of offices. He waved to his bailiff and Mrs. Berna Lohrman, his secretary. He stopped by the desk of his law clerk to repeat what the man in the elevator had said. "Splendid morning, splendid!" he said, entering his chambers. For the next ten minutes those outside heard him gaily whistling a tune from *The Pirates of Penzance.* Suddenly all sounds ceased, followed by an insistent buzz for the law clerk, who entered and found the Judge looking as though he had passed through the valley of the shadow of death. "I cannot fathom," said Judge Hand, "why I allowed myself to care *what* that fellow thought of my opinion!"

No other federal judge has been on the bench as long as Judge Hand. President Coolidge appointed him to the Circuit Court in 1924, directly from the District Court for the Southern District of New York, where he had sat for fifteen years. Since 1939 he has held the title of senior judge, a matter of seniority. In the hierarchy of the federal judiciary, the ten Circuit Courts of Appeals and the Court of Appeals for the District of Columbia lie just below the Supreme Court, which rarely reviews a circuit-court decision unless it involves a constitutional problem or conflicts with decisions in another circuit. Circuit-court judges are appointed for life by the President with the consent of the Senate. Their salary is $17,500 a year.

Each morning Judge Hand walks four miles to work, leaving his home, a three-story brownstone on Manhattan's Upper East Side, precisely one hour before he is due at the courthouse. This daily walk has become a ritual, to which he attributes his general robustness. "I shall continue the practice," he has told a friend, "until that final morning when, fittingly, I shall fall backward head over heels down the courthouse steps." His cousin, Judge Augustus Noble Hand, two and a half years his senior, considers the walks a species of self-torture and is given to saying, "Learned wonders why his back sometimes hurts. Why shouldn't it, walking all that distance at his age?" Several of the other judges of the Circuit Court occasionally go along on the walks, but few men can survive the sheer speed of the journey. The other judges have been known to drop out of line, one by one, and jump into cabs, while Judge Hand ploughs ahead without so much as a glance behind.

In the courtroom Judge Hand's appearance is formidable even when he is totally relaxed. Those who appear before him testify that it is a broadening intellectual experience, often with shattering over-tones. Only the most hardy retain their composure, and once, during a Yale Law School moot court at which he presided, a prize student rose to address him, took one look and promptly keeled over in a dead faint. Lawyers have a habit of insisting that the case at bar either pre-sents special aspects of the law hitherto inapplicable or is open-and-shut on the basis of established doctrine. Judge Hand resists both tendencies with the air of a tolerant schoolmaster. As long as the argu-ment remains germane, he listens attentively, putting on and remov-ing heavy tortoise-shell glasses and leaning across the bench. But let the argument wander or become diffused in mists of rhetoric and he begins to wriggle and twist. Experienced attorneys, recognizing the storm warnings, hurry back to the point. To an attorney who persists in rambling he will say, "May I inquire, sir, what *are* you trying to tell us?" Spirited cross-questioning follows, during which the Judge attempts to reach the bedrock of the argument. Few things infuriate him more than what he calls the "meadows of easy assumptions," interruptions, or attempts to flatter the bench. "I need not remind the distinguished judges of the Second Circuit of the law in this case," an attorney once began, with a broad smile. Judge Hand shot forward in his chair, cutting him short. "You impute a knowledge of the law to this bench," he said, "which it does not possess." Suffering from an attorney in love with the sound of his own voice, the Judge will occa-sionally scribble a note of protest and slip it to a colleague on the bench. "John Marshall once said," read one of them, "that among the qualities of a great judge was the ability to look a lawyer straight in the eye and not hear one word he was saying."

Before writing a first draft of an opinion, Judge Hand calls in his law clerk and, thinking aloud, outlines the general pattern of his deci-sion. To clerk for Learned Hand is considered a signal honor among lawyers. All but a few of his law clerks have been former editors of the *Harvard Law Review;* each spring the dean of the Law School rec-ommends several applicants from whom the Judge selects one, who comes to him the fall after graduation. Judge Hand and his clerk plunge into a case together, the clerk looking up references and suggesting possible lines of reasoning. The relationship is highly informal. The Judge has no objection to his clerk's bringing a sandwich, say, into his chambers, but he does balk at the chewing of gum. The clerk has a private office but no phone, a contemptuous gesture on the Judge's part not toward the clerk but toward the telephone, which he considers a distracting factor in modern life. He feels that mobility tends to stimulate thought, and while discussing a case both he and the clerk pace rapidly back and forth across the room, in opposite directions, brushing past each other approximately every thirty seconds. "My feeling," the Judge will say, "is that plaintiff has suffered a grievance for which there should be a remedy, but a man's property is limited to the chattels which embody his invention." Then, as he whizzes by the clerk: "Sonny! We have come to a parting of the ways. I smell Spearmint again. Throw out that gum! . . . But amendment of the copyright law is not urged here. Come now, what do you think?" At the conclusion of the discussion the clerk, winded, retires to his office and orders are issued not to disturb the Judge.

Judge Hand writes three to four drafts of every decision, either hunched over his desk composing on long sheets of yellow foolscap or leaning back in his chair with a wooden writing board across his legs. "I write opinions with my life's blood," he often says. "I suffer, believe me, I suffer." He will write and rewrite steadily for hours, occasionally diverting his mind by walking to a wooden lectern in a far corner of the room and reading several pages of some nonlegal book which lies open there. For several weeks one summer he made his way, at odd intervals, through a life of Cromwell. While concentrating on a point of law, he appears to be affected by extrasensory perceptions, enabling him to be jarred by noises inaudible to the normal ear. "There's a dog barking its head off down on the street," he told his secretary one afternoon. The secretary had inner doubts that anyone could hear barking twenty-four floors above the street, but she nonetheless told Sherman, his bailiff, who went downstairs and could neither see nor hear a dog. The results of his inquiry were transmitted to the Judge, who looked pained. Fifteen minutes later he buzzed for Sherman. "I tell you I can't work with that dog barking," he said. "Here's ten dollars. Find the dog and buy him." Sherman again went downstairs and walked several times around the courthouse, cocking an ear. Faintly, in the distance, he heard a dog barking. Following the sound, he trapped his quarry, howling like mad in the rear of a bar and grill on the edge of Chinatown, three blocks away. "Judge Hand can't work," said Sherman, pointing to a tiny window near the top of the courthouse. Somewhat stunned, the proprietor muzzled the dog.

When reviewing an admiralty case the Judge is not satisfied merely to study the briefs and oral arguments. He keeps a compass and magnifying glass in his top desk drawer and his closet contains a complete set of maps of the waters adjacent to New York City. Whipping out the compass and spreading a map across his desk, he will squint for hours through his magnifying glass, checking with the compass the location of every spot mentioned. In deciding *Dauntless Towing Line v. Canal Lakes Towing Co.,* 140 Fed. 2nd 215, a matter of a collision between two barges, he wrote, "As usual the testimony as to the whistles is contradictory. . . . Perhaps the most reasonable estimate is that she first blew when somewhat east of buoy 3A, about 1,200 feet from the place of collision. The only testimony is that the mutual approach of the vessels was nine miles an hour; and if so, the signal must have been given nearly three minutes before collision (even if we disregard the slow bell of the *Calatco*). That was ample time for the *Dauntless* to go to starboard."

Each case presents to Judge Hand a new intellectual pursuit of freedom, admittedly an awesome task considering that liberty, as he has said, "is an essence so volatile that it will escape any vial, however corked." A lawyer once said of the Judge, "First he articulates his prejudices and then cancels them out. If he happens to reflect liberal sentiment—and he appears to a good deal of the time—it is only because he feels it to be the correct interpretation, not the popular one." These days a considerable number of the Judge's opinions deal with labor disputes. Inevitably he has been accused of being both pro- and anti-labor. He would appear to be neither. "Justice, I think, is the tolerable accommodation of the conflicting interests of society," he has said, "and I don't believe there is any royal road to attain such accommodations concretely."

The first of the Hands in America, John, left Kent, England in 1644 and landed at Southampton, Long Island. Shortly thereafter he be-

came one of the nine original settlers of Easthampton, a windswept
waste of moors and dunes. His estate consisted solely of a Bible, psalm
book, pistol, and sword. In 1792 the Hands trekked to Shoreham,
Vt., on the shores of Lake Champlain. Judge Hand's grandfather
Augustus attended the first law school in this country, Judge Gould's,
at Litchfield, Conn. He subsequently served in Congress, the New
York State Senate and on the State Supreme Court. Learned Hand was
born in Albany in 1872. He was christened Billings Learned Hand
but before he was thirty had dropped the name Billings in favor of
Learned, which is his mother's maiden name. "Nobody could possibly think of a nickname for Learned," he said at the time. His father,
Samuel, was a prominent attorney and sat for a time on the Court of
Appeals, the highest court in the state. Learned's closest childhood
companion was his cousin Augustus, who lived in Elizabethtown,
north of Albany in the Adirondacks. Learned spent his summers there,
mostly swimming and climbing mountains. Occasionally at night the
boys would sit behind the house in the light of a lantern, discussing
free will and predestination. "We early decided," Augustus Noble
Hand recalls, "that the problem was insoluble." During the winters
Learned corresponded regularly with his cousin. "For Christmas, I
got from Papa a set of books by Dumas," he wrote when he was
twelve, "and I have nearly finished *The Count of Monte Christo,*
which is bully, but mamma wont let me read it on Sunday which is a
great privation. . . . I stood 2 in my class in the semi-annual work. The
boy who stood head being 97 240/480. and I stood 97 227/480 he
being 13/480 ahead of me."

Learned followed Augustus to Harvard by two years, parted his
hair in the middle, sported a drooping mustache and a pointed black
beard and was known, from his appearance, as the "ancient
Mongolian." He bustled through college *summa cum laude,* majoring
in philosophy under Santayana, Royce and William James, becoming
an editor of the *Advocate,* a member of Phi Beta Kappa and Class Day
orator of the class of 1893. "We have come at last to the time when
we must put away childish things and think as men," he declaimed in
his oration, but he was uncertain of his next move. "I was perfectly
indeterminate," he says today. "I thought of sticking to philosophy,

but my cousin had moved along to the law school, and there were so many lawyers in the family—so I went, too." Although he became an editor of the *Harvard Law Review* and graduated with honors, the law and Learned were not perfectly mated. "He had a speculative train of thought," his cousin recalls, "and thinking based to a considerable extent on precedent did not particularly interest him." Within two years after graduation from law school he had become a partner in an Albany law firm, but he was not at peace with himself. "Many times I felt like putting a gun to my head," he has said. "Nothing but foreclosures, mortgages, settlement of estates. Everything was petty and formal. Nobody wanted to get *behind* a problem."

In 1902 he took two decisive steps: he married and moved to New York. His bride was the former Frances Fincke of Utica, a graduate of Bryn Mawr. Hand joined a Wall Street firm and bought the brownstone house where he lives today. Three daughters were born to the Hands. Essentially discontented with the practice of law, Hand nonetheless prospered. Older attorneys such as C. C. Burlingham and George Wickersham, President Taft's attorney general, recognized that his talents were primarily judicial. In 1909, at their instigation, Taft appointed Hand a federal district judge for the Southern District of New York. The new judge was thirty-seven. Within three years he had become an active Bull Mooser. "I knew this: we had to break away from the Hanna thing—the control of the nation by big business," he says now. He ran for chief justice of the New York Court of Appeals on the Progressive ticket in 1913 and was defeated. "He just stood up," his cousin recalls, "and was knocked down." He never again went into politics.

By and large, judges lead unspectacular lives. Their careers, like broad plateaus, are unmarked by gullies and hills. Day after day across the years the struggles and triumphs of Judge Hand—his growth and influence—have been matters of the mind and spirit and therefore immeasurable. You cannot point to a judge as you would to a general and say, "He won *that* battle." Yet, as Hand once said of Cardozo, judges possess "a power greater than the power of him who ruleth a city." Many students of Judge Hand's work feel that his public addresses and articles in law journals have been among his greatest contributions. In them he has given expression to some of his deepest feelings on law and life and more particularly to his thoughts on the meaning of freedom. "We were wrong," he told a group of lawyers some years ago, "in supposing that native intelligence or stupidity have much to do with the workings of democracy or the gift of liberty. It is a question of the habit, so hard to acquire, of detachment in forming beliefs, in the end of a character of a people, not of its brains. A group of pretty dull men can manage fairly well, if they be disposed to suspend judgment where they do not know the facts, but nothing— I think you will agree—is more exasperating than a group of clever disputants each concealing behind his front of argument determined and uncompromising convictions which no evidence can touch."

He reiterated this theme in May 1944, when he led 150,000 newly naturalized citizens in the pledge to the flag at the "I Am An American Day" ceremonies in New York's Central Park. One million four hundred thousand persons attended, including Mrs. Hand, who sat behind the French horn of the Fire Department Band. They heard him formulate what many people still consider one of the finest definitions of liberty uttered by a living American, when he said, in part: "The spirit of liberty is the spirit which is not too sure that it is right. The spirit of liberty is the spirit which seeks to understand the minds of other men and women. The spirit of liberty is the spirit which weighs their interests alongside its own without bias. The spirit of liberty remembers that not even a sparrow falls to earth unheeded. The spirit of liberty is the spirit of Him who, near two thousand years ago, taught mankind that lesson it has never learned, but has never quite forgotten; that there may be a kingdom where the least shall be heard and considered side by side with the greatest." Though not a newspaper quoted his remarks, word of the speech rapidly spread. Several months later, as the result of reprints in newspapers and magazines, it had been read by an audience conservatively estimated at twenty-five million.

In former years when the work of the court was completed, the Judge and his wife often made summer trips to Europe, the Judge racing through chateaux, libraries, and museums at the rate of approximately a dozen a day. Returning to the U.S., he observed customs regulations so scrupulously that he once declared an old pair of shoes on the grounds that they had been resoled and heeled in Europe. Now, at the end of court sessions, the Judge leaves promptly for Cornish, New Hampshire, where he has a summer place called Low Court. He spends his days reading or tramping through the woods. In the evenings he puts on a white apron and helps Mrs. Hand with the dishes.

His New York home is high-ceilinged and comfortable, dominated on the lower floor by a long, narrow library containing several thousand books, including a large number of highly technical volumes of chemistry, physics, and geography. Judge and Mrs. Hand have four grandsons and three granddaughters. Their youngest daughter, Constance, is married to Newbold Morris, former president of the New York City Council and a member of the City Planning Commission.

Judge Hand's children have long been astounded at the duality of his nature: self-discipline and dedication to work on one hand, ability to relax thoroughly on the other. When they were young, they waited for him to come home each evening from the courtroom. Crouched on the second-floor landing, they learned to recognize his footsteps as he walked down Sixty-fifth Street and put a heavy bronze key in the front door. "If father entered the hall quietly and came silently up the stairs we knew he had problems and promptly dispersed," one of his daughters recalls. "If he were whistling or singing, we would tumble into his room for a story." The Judge would often reward them with an episode from *Br'er Rabbit*. "Lippity-lop, lippity-lop," he would say, hopping across the room. Or he might recount a chapter in the history of a blowzy character called Marge, a figment of his imagination. Marge, who has been involved in outrageous encounters with the law for more than thirty years, is well meaning but cannot avoid trouble. These days, she is in constant demand by the Judge's grandchildren, who also like to watch him place a wastebasket over his head and leap around the room like an Indian. "You do not see one Indian," Newbold Morris says, "but a whole tribe." The Judge frequently performs as the Crooked Mouth Family. He lights a candle and, taking the part of each member of the family, from the largest to the smallest Crooked Mouth, tries to blow it out. He puffs and huffs, but the candle burns brightly. Finally he wets a finger and snuffs out the flame.

Judge Hand's closest friends have profound respect for his humor and for the vocabulary that embellishes it. "When he plays the role of William Jennings Bryan addressing a political meeting in Jersey City, he is simply fantastically good," Felix Frankfurter, an old friend, has said. Oliver Wendell Holmes relished his repertoire. Once, during a visit to Holmes with Frankfurter, Hand was prevailed upon to sing a ribald song of the sea, entitled *The Cabin Boy*. When they left Holmes, Hand turned to Frankfurter and said, "I fear the old man thinks I am a mere vaudevillian." On the contrary, Holmes in 1923 wrote to his perennial correspondent, Sir Frederick Pollock, that Hand was a man "whom I should like to see on our bench." That Judge Hand is not on the Supreme Court is a matter of keen disappointment to a large section of the American bar.

If Judge Hand has any feelings on this subject, they lie deeply within him. "If I were to do it over again," he told a friend visiting him in his chambers not long ago, "I think perhaps I would be a physicist—open new vistas, move in step with the world. You know, I used to hope that I might be able to garner a harvest of wisdom. That has turned out to be a mistake, for I cannot see much further into the tangle of life than I could fifty years ago. I'm less disappointed than I should have thought. Indeed, there is solace in a companionship where all are groping their way equally in the same fog."

November 1946

CHAPTER 2

PATIENCE AND FORTITUDE

Fiorello LaGuardia—"The Little Flower"—three-time Mayor of New York, noted labor reformer, was colorful, volatile, beloved by many, and immensely effective. He vigorously fought municipal sleaze, passionately advocated slum clearance, achieved a new city charter, added mightily to the beauty of the city through huge public works, loved to play fireman by wearing a fireman's hat, rode in a prowl car (not a limousine), and, during the war, used radio as a means of public persuasion: mainly railing against price gougers. He is fondly remembered for reading aloud, with flourishes, from the comic strip Dick Tracy, during a newspaper strike. I once lived across the street from Gracie Mansion, the Mayor's official residence, and on Sunday evenings, from my window, I had the delicious pleasure of watching the Mayor stir spaghetti in a huge pot.

WE'VE BEEN TOLD THAT LaGuardia's Sunday broadcasts have become an accepted institution in a great many New York homes, like Sunday papers on the living-room floor. He's been making them regularly since shortly after Pearl Harbor, 1 to 1:30 P.M., WNYC, 830 on your dial. The Mayor speaks directly from his desk at City Hall, and last week we were on tap for the broadcast, arriving a few minutes ahead of time and being shown into a palm-potted anteroom along with several other visitors. These were Mr. Jan Masaryk of Czechoslovakia, former Mayor and Mrs. Holling of Buffalo, Judge and Mrs. Sullivan of Buffalo, and a florid-faced gentleman named Carroll, a mining engineer from Prescott, Arizona, who happened to be in town. City Hall had a Sabbath silence broken only by certain noises from the Mayor's chamber. A radio was going, and so was the Mayor, on the telephone. "*Figaro ci, Figaro la,*" we heard through the walls. "Goddammit, I'm sick and tired of you fellows.". . . "*Figaro! Figaro! Figaro!*". . . "Why can't you get those prices down?". . . "*Feegaro!*" Silence. At two minutes to one, the Mayor's door swung open and the guests in the anteroom were swiftly ushered in, Mr. Masaryk taking a seat alongside His Honor, who was behind a microphone at his desk, and who looked surprisingly unruffled and well brushed. The rest of us ranged ourselves in a semicircle before him. LaGuardia smiled at Masaryk and Masaryk smiled back.

Promptly at one, the Mayor unbuttoned his coat and vest with a violent gesture, loosened his tie, and leaned toward the microphone. "Patience and fortitude! Berlin and Tokio!" he said, and was off. He was relatively calm at the start, dealing with such matters as official bickering in Washington and the dimout in New York. He occasionally glanced at an open folder before him, filled with pink slips bearing typed notes. About one-twelve, matters became tense. "Oh, fish! Oh, fish!" the Mayor said. "Well, I had my usual call today from Mr. Triggs, head of the OPA Fish Division. Triggs says the filet situation will clear up, and of course if Triggs says so I believe him, so we'll wait and see. [Glasses moved up high on forehead] Apples! Another beautiful black market's in the making, and as for snap beans, I've asked the OPA to be ready with information for wholesalers and retailers—no reason why they can't have the information. [Glasses back to nose] But go slow on buying those snap beans until next week, when the full crop comes in.... Oranges! Yes, I'm going to talk about oranges again. They spoof me, especially a bunch of cheap, dirty, low-down, lowlife politicians. Well, I won't go into it [glasses low on nose], but there's no reason why you can't buy oranges by the pound rather than by the dozen. I told my wife about this and she said she'd never done it before and I said well, you used to buy bananas by the dozen, and now you buy them by the pound. She said she'd never thought of that. [Face right in microphone] Again I warn you chicken dealers! I'm not fooling! No more monkey business!" And so it went until one twenty-eight, at which point the Mayor introduced Mr. Masaryk, who spoke briefly, remarking that the only good Nazi was a dead Nazi. Mr. LaGuardia then echoed this sentiment and, at 1:29:30, repeated, "Patience and fortitude!"

The other visitors filed out, but we stayed behind and managed to get a few words with the Mayor. He said that the pink chits served to remind him of matters to be mentioned. "They just say, 'Eggs seventy-two cents' and stuff like that," he told us. He comes down to City Hall around noon on Sundays in a police prowl car, after a hearty lunch at home, and works for about an hour on the broadcasts, mulling over topics mentioned on the chits. During the week, his secretaries place likely ideas in the folder. He gets the latest market quotations on apples, snap beans, eggs, and the like, right up to the last moment on Saturday. He has regular office hours on Sunday afternoons, we learned, but often lets visitors pile up in the anteroom, since he makes a practice of listening to WNYC's broadcast of the Brooklyn Museum concerts immediately following his own program. When we left, he was about to snap on the radio again. He looked as happy as a boy.

November 1943

CHAPTER 3

FRIENDS TALKING

IN THE NIGHT

How the world has changed! In my wildest dreams I cannot picture a Mayor of the City of New York spending a casual entire evening with a reporter, just talking away and never asking to review the piece or to put anything off the record. The evening was a glorious one, and a lesson in freedom of the press. Since I never use a tape recorder, I had to concentrate deeply on the Mayor's words. O'Dwyer was such a vivid, colorful, flowing conversationalist that I felt even the presence of notepaper would inhibit his style. I managed to scribble a few key phrases on a slip of paper under the table. For the rest, I relied on my memory.

EVER SINCE MAYOR O'DWYER TOOK OFFICE, I have been curious about what sort of person he is, and not long ago, thanks to a mutual friend and to a breathing spell between municipal crises, I had a chance to find out a little of what I wanted to know. My friend arranged for me to have dinner with the Mayor and a couple of his close associates. "One of those long, relaxed, and talky evenings that the General enjoys most," my friend said. Mayor O'Dwyer, he added, is unusually shy and introspective for a man in public life, but I would find that among cronies he talks freely and gaily. My friend set a date and said that the Mayor would expect me at City Hall between six and six-thirty.

I got down to City Hall about a quarter after six. It was my first visit since the last days of the LaGuardia administration, and the change in atmosphere was noticeable. Under LaGuardia, the Hall seemed electric. Secretaries addressed one another hurriedly, in low tones, the way spies talk in Hitchcock movies. Everybody gave the impression that he was carrying a message to Garcia, and everything appeared to be a matter of life or death. The other night, the people working in City Hall seemed just as busy as their predecessors but not so nervous. Secretaries walked, rather than ran, down the corridors and through the doorways, and held, rather than clutched, papers in their hands.

I found the Mayor's executive secretary, a short, redheaded, jovially pugnacious-looking young man named William Donoghue, at a huge desk covered with papers in a room next to the Mayor's office, and introduced myself. He said that the Mayor still had several people waiting to see him but that they wouldn't take very long. "Lord knows, the plans may change," Donoghue said, "but as of this minute the three of us will eat at the New York Athletic Club with Dave Martin, in his private office. Dave is one of the General's oldest friends, and he's the manager of the club, and the General really enjoys going there. Relaxes him." I sat down with a newspaper in a corner of Donoghue's office. It was dark outside, and a high wind was blowing through City Hall Park. I could see the trees swaying, and every now and then a heavy gust rattled Donoghue's windows. Then it began to rain very hard and big drops splashed against the glass.

After five or ten minutes, Mayor O'Dwyer stuck his head in the door. His coat and tie were off, his sleeves were rolled up, and he was smoking a big cigar. He seemed shorter, and a good deal broader, especially in the shoulders, than his pictures indicate. He looked like a man who had put in a hard day at the office. At first glance, his face appeared fleshy and somewhat worn, but when I glanced a second time, particularly at his sensitive eyes and mouth, I could see a youthful, humorous expression. "In the clear, Bill," he said to Donoghue. "I'll be ready in a minute. Just have to put on my coat and tie." He walked over and shook hands with me. "I could stand a good meal and a good chin," he said. He went back into his office and reappeared wearing a hat and a trench coat. He called to Donoghue and me, and we started down the corridor. I noticed what looked like ragged pin holes in the shoulder straps of his coat, and I asked if it was the one that he had worn in the Army. "The very same," he said. "Best coat I ever owned, so I just took the stars off the shoulders." A guard told the Mayor that, because it was raining, his car was parked at a basement door at the east end of the building. "We don't want you to get your feet wet," the guard said. "And many thanks," said the Mayor. We went down a flight of stairs, left the building by a side door, and got into a black seven-passenger Cadillac. A man wearing a gray felt hat was sitting stiffly at the wheel.

As we started uptown, the Mayor sat back and looked out at the glistening wet streets. "Nothing gloomier on a night like this than a jail," he said after a while, "unless it's a ballpark. Oh, but a jail is gloomy on a rainy night!" The Mayor's voice seems both hard and soft. At first, it sounds somewhat rasping and declamatory, but as you listen, it gradually assumes a pleasant, dreamy, far-off, rhythmic quality.

"Bill," he said, "you remember I was telling you the other day how I was sitting at my desk—some people had just left the office—and for some reason or other, I can't figure why, I started to think of Big Matty Cullane, who was on the force when I was."

"I do, General," said Donoghue.

"Well," said the Mayor, "I have just this minute thought of Big Nell Flaherty—the thought comes right down the years—and that brings Big Matty to mind again. Matty Cullane," he said to me, "was one of the sweetest, gentlest, loveliest men that ever lived. He was six feet two, and loose. Not tight and knotted, like some big men, but loose. When I knew Matty, I was a rookie cop along the Brooklyn waterfront—Forty-third Street and Fourth Avenue—and it was tough, with the Kid Cheese Gang and all the rest making life uncomfortable. Lots of cops had been beaten up by the Kid Cheese Boys. They lured them into doorways or staged fake fights in barrooms or turned in false alarms, to bring the cops running, and then they'd jump them. Well, Matty Cullane was put on the beat and informed of the difficulties of the route. So he starts down the street one day and a young tough steps up on a corner and snaps his fingers in Matty's face and says, 'Why, you great big Irish flatfoot!,' and then ducks into a doorway, Matty right behind. Of course, the gang is waiting in the doorway for Matty, and you're thinking he's stupid, but hidden in his pocket is the short billy, not the long one, and a murderous weapon, and in about seven minutes there is a considerable pile of young men lying in the street and several lads crumpled on the stairway and one or two legging it across the roof of the building, Matty in hot pursuit. Next thing, Matty has them by the ears and is dragging them down the stairs, clippity-clop, clippity-clop, and he throws them onto the pile of their colleagues on the street. At this point, a gentle old lady walks past and notices the debris and says, 'Officer,' she says, 'please do not be unkind to these boys,' and Matty says, 'Pardon me, lady, but at this moment I am not interested in the emotion of sympathy.'" The car stopped outside the Athletic Club. "When we get upstairs, I'll tell you about Nell Flaherty," the Mayor said.

Dave Martin, a solemn, grayish man of fifty, was waiting for the Mayor outside his offices, on the twelfth floor. We followed him into a room looking west over Columbus Circle. It contained a flat-top desk, several floor lamps, and a few easy chairs. The Mayor instantly removed his suit coat and tie, settled into a large chair near a window, and leaned back, putting his feet on the sill. The rest of us sat down around the room. A waiter entered, went right to the Mayor, and shook hands with him.

"Paddy, at the bar, wants to mix you one of his martinis," the waiter said.

"One of Paddy's martinis is like two of anyone else's," said the Mayor. "Tell him to take it easy."

Donoghue and I ordered a drink, and Martin said he'd pass.

"Now, for supper," said the waiter, "why not eat steak for a change, instead of filet of sole all the time?"

"That's right," said Martin. "A steak will do you good."

The Mayor pondered the matter a moment. "Well, it's a party," he said. "I'll take a steak." The rest of us said we'd have the same.

As the waiter left the room, the Mayor turned to Martin. "Dave," he said, "I've been talking about Matty Cullane and Big Nell Flaherty." Martin smiled and nodded. "Now, Big Nell Flaherty also lived in Brooklyn," continued the Mayor, "and she also was six feet two, but that's not so good for a woman, and as a result Nell took to drink. One drink, and Big Nell was flat in a doorway, where she slept like a pure, pink, newborn babe, and dreamed, I should imagine, of love and affection. All the cops knew Big Nell, and a cop would walk up and try to wake her and get her on her feet, and she'd reach up and bop! down he'd go. Another cop would hear the commotion and come running, and bop! down he'd go." The Mayor sat up straight and made a broad gesture with his cigar. "Police records reveal," he said, "that Big Nell was never taken into custody by less than six officers of the law until her seventy-fourth year, when, one night, it required merely two policemen to bring her to court, and one of the two was Big Matty Cullane. She stood before the magistrate, who inquired, 'Do you desire justice, Nell, or do you wish to go to Special Sessions?' 'Last time you told me that,' said Nell, 'it resulted in thirty days.' Well, Matty speaks up and says, 'Your Honor, I will take care of the lady,' and the judge says, 'Case dismissed.' Matty takes her out and he says, 'Nell, you're not getting any younger. Witness the fact that it required only two cops to bring you in. I'm taking you over to the hospital and getting you a good cleaning out.' 'I want no sympathy from no cop,' says Nell. But Matty prevailed and Nell went to the hospital for a good cleaning out, and two days later she died. Matty was told about it and he felt very bad. 'I killed her,' he always said. 'It wasn't the humiliation of having two cops bring her in, it was the cleaning out.'" The Mayor was silent for a moment or two. "But I don't know why I should be thinking about Big Nell tonight," he said. "Or Big Matty, either, for that matter."

The waiter brought us our drinks and wheeled in a table all set for dinner. The Mayor sipped his martini. "Oh, but that Paddy makes a lethal martini," he said. "My compliments to him. Speaking of bartenders," the Mayor said to me, "I was one myself once, you know—several years after I came here from Ireland and before going on the force. I was mostly at the service bar in hotels, working downstairs in my shirtsleeves and mixing drinks to be sent to the rooms. Well, I was working at the Plaza one night—I can see it now, a night just like tonight, the city a sheet of rain—and I was substituting at the big bar upstairs, in the Oak Room. Hardly anybody in the place, a few quiet drinkers drifting through, the Park outside like a melody in the rain. Now, there were three people seated at a table in one corner, and they were Arnold Daly, the actor; Jim Corbett, the fighter; and John McGraw, of the Giants. The evening droned along, every now and then a waiter coming over to the bar and asking for two more glasses of alcoholic beverage and one nonalcoholic—that was for Jim Corbett—and the three of them just chinning away, the way we are now, just the quiet hum of friends talking in the night, when suddenly there was a hullabaloo, the way a summer storm roars up, with thunder and lightning, and I look across and the peaceful scene has become animated. Daly is standing up and waving his arms and shouting at the top of his lungs, 'Tomorrow, and tomorrow, and tomorrow, creeps in this petty pace from day to day,' and John McGraw eyes him and says, 'Aw, *shut up!*,' and Jim Corbett, the pugilist, rises and stretches out his hands and cries, 'Gentlemen, gentlemen!'"

"Dinner's ready, General," said the waiter, "and I've brought some clams for a starter." We moved over to the table.

"Another martini?" asked the waiter.

"Oho, no," said the Mayor, "but I'd like a glass of beer."

We finished our clams and went to work on the steaks. The Mayor ate slowly, and talked a good deal between bites. "Wish you could have seen the *nouveaux riches* swarming into this town when I was tending bar," he said. "The cattlemen, the copper kings, the big plainsmen, the sports, all with buckets of money, and they didn't know how to behave in a great city, especially toward the help. I fell to thinking about some of those snoots just the other day, when I went into the

Vanderbilt Hotel for lunch. I worked there once, and some of the people I worked with are still there. The hatcheck woman, Mary, came out to say hello, and made a fuss over me, and then, my God, if old Barney wasn't still there! Today he's head elevator starter, but in my time he was checking hats and coats, and seeing him reminded me, as I say, of the snoots, and especially of Diamond Jim Brady. I'd like to get my hands on the fellow who wrote that movie about Diamond Jim, because he was a beglittered, overstuffed pig, with his diamond-headed canes, and his cuff links and stickpins all in little animal shapes. One night he marches into the Vanderbilt with the famous Dolly Sisters in tow. One of these Dolly Sisters always wore a live monkey around her neck in place of a fur piece, and she stands in front of Barney at the hatcheck window and says, 'Boy, check this,' and Barney says, 'Madam, it would please me to oblige, but there is no guarantee this monkey is housebroke and I cannot place it on the rack with all these fine furs. It will have to be put in the basement, where the dogs are kept.' At the sound of the word 'dogs,' the Dolly Sister looks as though she will fall back on the lobby floor in a faint, and Diamond Jim waves his diamond-headed stick and hollers for the management. Lord bless him, that manager sat in his office and wouldn't stir until he had analyzed the facts as brought to him, and he decides for Barney. Then he goes into the lobby. 'Fire that man!' shouts Brady, pointing at Barney, and the manager bows from the waist and says, 'Yes, sir,' and then he whispers to Barney to lay low in the basement and keep off the upper floors for a day or two, until the storm blows over. Now, the funny thing is that years later, when I'm a magistrate in Brooklyn, who comes before me but old Barney. Parked his car on a bridge. Had a ticket. I looked at Barney and thought the Lord God in Heaven has been waiting for years for a chance to reward you for telling that Dolly Sister to put the monkey with the dogs, and I found extenuating circumstances and dismissed the case, and I've always felt that justice was done."

The Mayor pushed his chair back from the table, lighted another cigar, and blew several clouds of smoke toward the ceiling.

"You're looking well," Martin said to him.

"You know," said the Mayor, "I think I'm on top of this job—out of the woods. Came out of the woods six months after I took office."

"General," said Donoghue, "I think you came out of the woods before six months."

"You're wrong, Bill," said the Mayor. "I came into the clear around July. At the beginning, so many things happened all at once. I was afraid of a postwar crime wave, and the force was sadly depleted. Other city departments were understaffed, and not all due to draft shortages, either. We had the tugboat strike, the transport workers' problem, the whole business of Idlewild Airport, a Health Department that wasn't everything it was cracked up to be." He rose and started walking slowly around the room. "I'm far from satisfied," he said, "but we haven't had the postwar crime wave. We've added to the force. Wallander is a good man, and I leave him alone; don't tell him how to run his business. The department's clicking *these* days, all right."

"Swell," said Martin.

"Moreover," said the Mayor, "we've got raises for some city employees. I sat up all one night working over raises, and later some of my so-called friends insisted I had been kicked into it, never would have had the idea on my own."

"That sort of talk comes along with everything else," said Donoghue.

"Right," said the Mayor. "Same as when we were getting a new Health Commissioner. I'll not forget one of the papers in this town going after me savagely, saying I didn't want an honest, unpolitical Health Department, accusing me of turning down one of the best public-health men in the country. Well, a simple phone call to the man in question would have proved how really anxious I had been to make him Commissioner. He turned down the job for reasons of his own. Later, when a group of public-health men gave me a panel of selected names, I looked over the list, and most of them were from out of town, and I said, 'Hell, gentlemen, why can't we have a Commissioner who knows how to drop a nickel in the slot and reach Flatbush?' A man, in other words, who in addition to scientific knowledge knows something of this city and its particular problems. You need honesty and more to run a good city department. Why, when I came into office, bread was being made for schoolchildren by prisoners on Riker's Island, but there wasn't a cake of soap on the Island and nobody was washing his hands. The restaurants all over town were filthy! The city cannery was a pigpen! Well, we've cleared up these things, and our Commissioner knows how to reach Flatbush, and we spent sixty thousand dollars exploding that stinkweed, ragweed."

The Mayor moved his chair back to the table, sat down, and took several sips of coffee. His cigar, I noticed, had gone out. "Those first days in office," he said. "They were uneasy for all concerned." He relighted his cigar. "But that's water over the dam," he said suddenly. "Over the dam. We want a happy city. Better schools. Those old Civil War firetraps are ghastly. We want textbooks that give children a sense of their city and a practical understanding of what democracy is all about. Racial discrimination has plagued our maturity, and we just can't have it. You know, Dave, some of the old neighborliness has gone. That's natural growth in a town, I guess, but there's a large area of tolerance left and it must be retained. God, we've got our faults, but they're not inhuman ones. Nobody's dragged from his bed at night, nobody's told what to think, no secret police. It must be left that way, for black and white and Jew and Gentile."

"What else makes a happy city?" I asked.

"Well-run departments," said the Mayor. "Good sanitation. Plenty of playgrounds. Cheap transportation to and from work, and plenty of it. Good labor-management relations. Room to park cars. And friendliness. Lots of people would have us believe this town is loaded with thugs, racketeers, gamblers. I say it's a friendly city. It's been friendly to me."

"Remember what you were saying to that jewellers' convention the other night?" said Donoghue.

The Mayor laughed. "Came to me on the spur of the moment," he said.

"What was it?" asked Martin.

"Nothing," said the Mayor. "I just said that we people who live in

New York like to pull out our tray, with all our good things on it—our people and parks and museums—pull it out just like a jeweller, I told them, and show off our beauties."

"I like that," said Donoghue.

"Well," said the Mayor, "it's not the fashion to be sentimental, but I've seen a good many places on this earth—I've seen the cities of the Old World, and I've shipped to South America as an ordinary seaman, and I've been to every state in this union except Washington—and I come back here every time, because it's one hell of a town. Moreover, it's a waterfront town, and waterfronts and waterways are part of our heritage, and part of our future, too. I've no quarrel, God knows, with big airplane runways and the like, but show me the town with a great, wide harbor and a river navigable to Troy. Baltimore almost stole our thunder in the old days, but the smart old boys understood the situation and built the Erie Canal."

The Mayor put his elbows on the table and his chin in his hands. He sighed. "I'm fifty-six," he said, "and when you're fifty-six, you're headed down the other side of the slope. I often turn to Yeats and Sean O'Casey for comfort. But it's hard to tell what counts, what's important, and you certainly can't tell at the time. Years back, when I was a young lad, I was a hod carrier working on the McAlpin Hotel, and we all joined a small hod carriers' union, and who could have predicted it would become very important in this community? So it all adds up to this—you want to give the kids a chance to grow in their own way, in a democratic world, to make their own choices, to live out their lives without regimentation, and to transmit that heritage to their kids. I'm not fooling myself. It's a fluke when a youngster comes here with a couple of bucks in his pocket and people are friendly and he becomes Mayor. But the chance must be left open." Martin and Donoghue nodded vigorously.

"One thing I do know," the Mayor went on. "I don't want to be one of those ex-Mayors, with people looking down the street and saying, 'My God, here comes old Bill O'Dwyer, once was Mayor of New York, what job does *he* want from us?,' and then ducking into an alley or an ashcan. No, I'll take to the highway of the world or follow the sun across the horizon."

The Mayor got up and began to put on his tie and coat. "It's time to go home," he said. "I've talked a good deal, and yet there's a good deal still to be talked about. Sometimes I think the human values are the only real values. Thought about that one night a couple of weeks ago, when I was out with some dear friends—J. Fred Coots, who wrote *She Walks in Beauty,* and Walter Shirley, the real-estate man. We were in the country and we walked onto a lawn. It was a clear and beautiful night and the sky was a bright bowl of stars. The moon was a thin sliver behind the trees. The wind blew a bit and the boughs of the trees were outstretched, as the poet said, in prayer. And we got to talking about the olden times, when we were young fellows together in Brooklyn, and Coots said, 'Say,' he said, 'do you remember Mike O'Sheehan, old O'Sheehan that played the violin and had the big ears?' And everybody nodded and said, 'Do *we* remember old O'Sheehan that played the violin and had the big ears!,' and it was like yesterday and we were youngsters again and you couldn't figure how the years had passed. But none of us *really* remembered old O'Sheehan, wouldn't know him if we saw him. We knew him and we didn't, and yet we knew he must have played the violin and had big ears, and what more do you need to know?"

December 1946

from THE IDEA IS EVERYTHING

A prominent Norwegian Labor Party official, often described as an "old-fashioned Social Democrat," Trygve Lie had a harrowing escape from the Nazi invasion of his country, was foreign minister of the Norwegian government in exile, and was a compromise candidate between East and West when he became the first Secretary-General of the United Nations. He fell into disfavor with the Russians when he supported the United Nations' intervention in Korea. Lie's problems have faced every Secretary-General.

−I−

UNDER THE TERMS OF HIS five-year compact with the United Nations, Trygve Lie, the Secretary-General, feels honor bound to maintain the international point of view. If any national thoughts rise into his consciousness, he does his best to toss them out. In his official lexicon, every country is the equal of every other country, provided it is a dues-paying member of his organization. As far as Lie is concerned, El Salvador is as good as you are, whoever you are. In his eyes, there is no difference between Sir Alexander Cadogan in his Bond Street suit and an Arab sheik in his burnoose. In a world composed exclusively of national states, all extremely jealous of their prerogatives, Lie's job is not an easy one. It is further complicated by the inescapable fact that, like other men, Lie was born in a specific sovereign area, or "country." He is a Norwegian. Secretary-General or not, he finds Norway popping into his mind with awkward frequency. There are, for example, no world dishes. Nobody has as yet concocted a cosmic stew. Often, when Lie returns home at night after a hard day at the office tussling with world problems, he sits down to a plate of *rakørret,* a thoroughly Norwegian dish. *Rakørret* is trout that have been kept in a barrel until they begin to smell. Norwegians love *rakørret,* and why not? Lie lives in a typically suburban home in Forest Hills, but in cold weather he keeps his house at no more than an even fifty-eight degrees, which is way below the Forest Hills average. A sheik would probably freeze to death in Lie's house. Some of Lie's neighbors would undoubtedly catch a cold. Lie can't help it. He is a Norwegian, and Norwegians prefer cold houses. No matter how assiduously Lie may try to think in world terms, he still enjoys a nip of aquavit more than any other drink. Lie the internationalist is constantly bumping into Lie the Norwegian, just as the United Nations keeps colliding with its component parts. "What's happening to Lie is happening to all of us," a United Nations official says. "The world has a split personality, and Lie, as Secretary-General, naturally has one of the monumental splits."

Lie could easily be mistaken for a man without a care in the world, or any country thereof. He is fifty-one, tall, portly, and florid, and has the look of the traditional jolly, playful, roughhouse, doesn't-know-his-own-strength zoo bear. He walks lightly, almost airily, on the balls of his feet. Hundreds of tiny lines web the skin around his eyes, giving the impression that he has done more than one man's share of laughing. Sometimes, taking advantage of his privilege of attending any meeting of any United Nations organ (the UN term for the General Assembly and any council and committee), he leaves his office at Lake

Success and visits a session of, say, the Security Council or the Economic and Social Council. Visitors to these meetings sometimes remark that they feel comforted by his presence. A moment before, listening to the delegate of one nation hurling invective at the delegate of another nation, they may have wondered whether the world would blow up before supper, but Lie's arrival quickly makes the world seem reasonably united again. Lie, relaxed, placid, almost detached, always looks as though he had everything under control. His face usually bears an expression denoting neither pain, impatience, nor despair. In February, 1946, in London, shortly after he was elected Secretary-General, he sat quietly through the early sessions of the Security Council. The wartime harmony of the great powers appeared, somewhat unexpectedly, to be cracking up, but the more irreconcilable their expressed views became, the more beatific Lie looked. Many delegates, inspecting their stolid Secretary-General, felt that he had a startling unsensitivity. "I found myself staring at Mr. Lie," one delegate has since remarked, "and I was reminded of the duck with the water flowing from its back." Most of the time, Lie is actually suffering a bottomless sadness, and on that occasion his outward calm belied an inner turbulence rivaling that of Vesuvius. "Those first sessions stunned me," Lie later told an acquaintance. "Here were the victorious allies banded together in a world organization dedicated to peace, and they were fighting among themselves almost before the sound of the last shot had died away. I could not believe my ears. I could not understand it. I kept looking from one face to another and saying to myself, 'Where are the great men, where are the statesmen, where are the people with vision who will save this thing?'"

Lie is acutely aware that the national-mindedness of sovereign states could wreck his business. He is also troubled by his own duality; he has an intense devotion to the concept of an undivided world and at the same time a firm allegiance to one country of that world. He suspects that his personal problem may be the central problem of our time. Few men have tried so diligently to cultivate a world view. It is an uphill fight. During the first session of the General Assembly at Flushing Meadow, Lie's request for a twenty-seven-million-dollar budget ran into difficulties at a committee meeting. Several committee members felt that the new world organization was proving to be much too expensive. Lie attended the meeting and listened silently to the discussion. To him, it seemed as though the committee members might find themselves turning the United Nations into a global bargain basement, and he asked for the floor. Aroused, he was a formidable figure. The blood rushed to his face. He nervously rubbed the webby skin beneath his eyes. His huge shoulders looked as though they were going to burst through his coat. Puffing like a wind machine, he delivered an impassioned argument, and, much to his dismay, found himself discussing the United Nations in national terms. "I come from a small country with a small budget," he heard himself saying. "As a Norwegian, I know the value of money. We are cautious with expenditures. We live within our incomes. Thrift is my watchword. As a Norwegian, I would never ask for more than I felt we needed." Lie's national approach easily carried the day for his international budget. It also evoked from the committee members a series of long and embarrassing tributes to Norway. The American member praised the character and industry of those sturdy Viking sons who settled in our own Midwest. The Canadian member extolled the husbandry of the Norwegians, who were in large part responsible for the rich and golden wheat fields of Saskatchewan and Alberta. "It was a most strange session," a member of the United Nations Secretariat who was present said not long ago. "All of us, including Mr. Lie, realized that his arguments were old hat, but on the other hand none of us had been educated to put forth any up-to-date ones. This generation is trying like hell to get away from its grandmother, and, believe me, it's a struggle!"

October 1947

CHAPTER 5

SCULLING ON THE SCHUYLKILL

This Talk of the Town piece portrays the manic quality of an old-fashioned, knockdown, no-holds-barred political convention.

OUR DELEGATION TO THE Republican National Convention consisted of Mr. Stanley, who hung around Philadelphia for a day and then took a train to Hot Springs for a deserved rest. We received the following memo from him, written in his porch chair:

"Having wonderful time, wish you were here. Coming along as well as can be expected, but still dizzy when I try to walk. Philly pretty much of a blur. Got pushed into lobby of Bellevue-Stratford at 10 A.M. Reached elevators at ten-fourteen. Pushed into elevator at ten-thirty. Pushed out at fourteenth floor. 'May I inquire what type of razor blade you used this morning?' asked a man standing in front of the elevator. Told the man Gillette, and was pushed into down elevator, arriving back in lobby at ten-thirty-six. Nothing gained, nothing lost. Swept up by brass band headed for Stassen headquarters, at rear of lobby, walking alongside large lady trumpet player, who whispered, 'MacArthur just flew in from Japan!' Man even larger than lady trumpet player shoved her aside and handed me pamphlet titled 'Presenting Some Facts on the Gang from Michigan.' Pushed into Stassen headquarters at ten-fifty. 'Right this way, Commissioner!' a little lady without a trumpet cried, and placed me in a reception line, where I shook hands for an hour with string of very nice people, mostly family types. Was called Governor thirteen times, Senator four times, and turned down the nomination twice. Terrific pressure from behind took me up stairs to second floor, where a man solemnly pinned on my lapel a bronze medal, dangling from a red, white, and blue ribbon, and engraved 'Newsreel Operator.' 'With this, doors open,' the man said. A door opened and I found myself in taxi with group of Landon rooters, all very nice people. 'What newsreel company you with?' someone asked. I told him Gillette. We disgorged before Independence Hall. Visited the Hall and some adjoining buildings, saw Washington's Masonic apron, some clean-cut and quiet rooms where the Senate and House of Representatives met from 1790 to 1800, several splendid glass decanters, and the Liberty Bell. Crack in bell is bigger than you'd think.

"Shook off the Landon rooters and walked down Chestnut Street. Alone at last. Pondered whether I should have accepted nomination. Terrible responsibility. Ran into crowd surrounding man with pins and pennants. 'William Howard Taft buttons, first-class curio, fifty cents,' he said. Was pushed straight through Wanamaker's Grand Court into taxi with Taft supporters, very nice people. Pushed out at Benjamin Franklin Hotel, handed cardboard four-leaf clover attached to blue ribbon reading, 'Taft Greeters,' and into room with the Senator, who was holding press conference. He said he heartily endorsed the platform but hadn't read it thoroughly. 'Tsina aid, Senata?' cried a Chinese newspaperman from the rear of the hall. 'Wha-at?' said Taft. 'Senata endorse Tsina aid, economic, military?' elaborated the Chinese newspaperman. 'I'm for China aid,' said the

Senator. 'Turkey, Greece?' shouted a swarthy gentleman. 'I'm for
Turkey, Greece,' said the Senator. 'Thank you, Senator,' said another
newspaperman, and the crowd rose to leave. A man went past with a
walkie-talkie. 'The crowd is now rising to leave,' he said into the
walkie-talkie. Into taxi with fellow newsreel operators, to Hotel
Warwick, where found Stassen seated on large bar alongside huge
Wisconsin cheese, holding press conference. Stassen heartily endorsed
the platform but said he hadn't read it thoroughly. Cheese at Stassen's
very good. Propelled out to street.

"At door of Bellevue-Stratford, stopped by man who asked, 'May I
inquire what type of razor blade you used this morning?' Was escorted
by four young ladies wearing Warren buttons into Dewey fashion
show in Grand Ballroom. Mrs. Dewey, in bottle green, entered box
overlooking stage, accompanied by Mrs. Worthington Scranton, Mrs.
Randolph Wilkes-Barre, and Mrs. Herbert Harrisburg. A Mrs. Hogan
introduced a Mrs. McMullan as 'the ringmaster of the Philadelphia
social circus.' Mrs. McMullan introduced the models. 'Wrinkle-proof
and washable shorts, delightful to relax in with a good book and a
nice man,' said Mrs. McMullan. Handed bottle of Pepsi-Cola by man
wearing Vandenberg cummerbund, and got whisked into back elevator, up to sixth floor, and into room thick with smoke. Met a senator,
and a senator's dog. Very nice dog. The senator was in a huddle with
two men, reading a note. 'Never heard of them,' said the senator,
handing the note to one of the men. 'But, Harry,' said the man, 'that's
where your wife said to meet her for supper.' The senator extended
his hand to me. 'Never saw you looking so well,' he said. 'How things
shaping up?' Pushed into elevator again. 'Want to read a beautiful letter?' asked a lady wearing a big purple orchid. There were tears in her
eyes. The letter was from General Wainwright, addressed to the delegates. Couldn't read the letter, because of too many people. Shoved
out at eighteenth floor and into another ballroom, face to face with
Governor Dewey, who wore a fixed smile and looked as though he
were being operated by strings. '. . . think of the platform?' someone
was asking. 'Looks good,' Dewey said, swinging to the right to shake
hands with three small boys, swinging front to write four autographs,

and swinging left to read eight messages handed him by aides. 'Ed Martin . . . good government . . . old friends . . . certain victory . . . breaking new ground,' said the Governor, swinging slowly from side to side. Caught the eight-twenty-three out of town. Good sleep on the way down."

July 1948

CHAPTER 6

HQ.

WE BLISSFULLY DISPATCHED our man Stanley to Mr. Dewey's headquarters, at the Hotel Roosevelt, on the Truman-Dewey election night. He returned to the office next afternoon, unshaven and rumpled:

Reached Roosevelt at 8:03. Cops, cops, cops, cops outside, cops on the stairs, cops inside. Lobby filling up with happy, buzzing citizens. Most ladies wearing orchids. Big, purple ones. Men well barbered. Aglow. Absolutely aglow. Went to rooms for press, on mezzanine. Sign by coatracks said, "No tipping." "On the house tonight," said check girl. Vast quarters for press, no stone unturned. Historic night. Room each for newsreels, radio men, photographers, wire services, television. Another room with nothing but tables and telephones. Telephones free. Pitchers of ice water all over the place. Not many press people around—too early—so made five or six phone calls. Wonderful feeling. Spotted George Sokolsky and Robert Considine outside in corridor, aglow, and realized pundits arriving, things getting under way. Nodded to Sokolsky. "Hello, Dick," he said. "What a night!" Went to big ballroom, also on mezzanine. More bunting than Fourth of July. Orchestra playing quiet dinner music at one side of ballroom. Hundreds of chairs facing big election-returns board. Room getting crowded. Boys in green jackets lettered "THE PHILIPS COMPANY — BEAUTIFUL SIGNS," putting paper numerals on hooks on big board. Returns coming in slowly. Ruddy-type man in dress suit watching returns in doorway, smoking biggest cigar in the world. Asked him how things shaping up. Blew thick cloud and said, "Early big-city returns for Truman, natch. Wait for the grass roots, boy. Have a cigar." Gave me second-biggest cigar in the world. Back to press rooms and made more phone calls. Press rooms getting crowded. Sokolsky center of jovial group. Spotted me and said "Hello, Paul!" Blew smoke at him and went to watch television sets. Gallup talking, impressive, calm, collected. Gallup replaced by Winchell, wearing hat. Real newspaperman. No nonsense tonight, no amateurs. Pearson followed Winchell on screen, also wearing hat. A Lee. Pearson predicting like crazy man. (How he know so much, anyway?)

Back to ballroom. Filled now. Healthy crowd, well rested. Boy rushed to board with new figures. Dewey forging ahead in Kansas. Now two hundred ahead in Kansas. Cheers from crowd. Man who gave me cigar slapped my back. "This is it, boy!" he said. "Grass roots coming in. Have a cigar." Took third-biggest cigar in the world. Man also handed me engraved card. "Special invitation to hear returns on second floor," he said. "Use it, boy." Used it. Found dressy group of men and women watching television sets in fine suite of rooms. Quiet group. Seemed cautious. Selected rye highball from liquor tray, took it to empty place on sofa, and picked up pile of Tuesday's newspapers. Read Danton Walker column ("... Dewey's first official act as President-elect will be to name a new Secretary of State ..."). Read John O'Donnell column ("... most important problem facing the Republic in the next few days is how Dewey and Truman will work out a method of handling our foreign affairs until Jan. 20 rolls around ..."). Read column in *Journal-American* by George Rothwell Brown ("The President has been unable to overtake Gov. Dewey in the conclusive area of electoral votes, and these, under the

Constitution, are what count . . ."). Brown had something there. Back to ballroom. Ballroom restive. Boy rushed over to blackboard with flash. Dewey ahead by 2,800 in Philadelphia. Cheers. Carbon statement from Brownell: ". . . so we conclude . . . that Dewey and Warren are elected." Sokolsky walked past, said, "Evening, Charles." Some of the glow gone. Gallup on television again. Looked older. Back to ballroom. Orchestra playing "When Irish Eyes Are Smiling." No eyes smiling. Newsreel men on balcony asked crowd to cheer wildly for news-of-victory pictures. Crowd cheered wildly on second try, settled back quietly. Man in dress suit still standing by door. Looked hurt. "Boy," he said, "here's a ticket for very private party in Mr. Hogan's room. Closest friend of Governor. Use it." Used it. Inside, Henry J. Taylor, pundit, sitting by radio, head in hand. Nobody speaking. William Gaxton entered, smiling. Wiped it off. Hogan very serious. "Can't understand it," he said. Told him to wait for grass roots. He seemed grateful. Lady in pink organdie and hair like curry powder said, "He didn't campaign right. Too damn respectable." Taylor departed clasping and unclasping hands. Large gentleman in tuxedo said, "It's what you call winning the hard way." Mild laughter. Back to ballroom. People putting on coats, consulting timetables. Boys in green jackets mostly standing around, putting up very few figures. Sat down beside man who looked like Truman. Thought maybe it *was* Truman. "Tom's dying by inches," he said. "Have a cigar." Rumor Governor coming down to speak. Sat there two hours. No Governor. Edwin F. Jaeckel, Dewey adviser, appeared on balcony with foolish grin. Lowell Thomas walked through ballroom. Same grin. Back to press rooms. Sokolsky clamping hat on head, putting on coat. Didn't recognize me. Definitely time to go home.

November 1948

When I left the hotel at a late hour, Dewey had not yet conceded. I wrote my story, caught a brief shut-eye, and, propelled by some beckoning instinct, went back to the Roosevelt shortly after nine in the morning. Dewey quite suddenly appeared in the ballroom and mounted a deserted platform. The floor of the cavernous room was still littered with hundreds of airless, dead balloons. The Governor was obviously exhausted, red-eyed, and monumentally disappointed. But the manner of his concession has remained vividly in my mind. He had fought hard and, in some instances, nastily for the job. But now, in the presence of a few reporters and friends, he conceded with courage and dignity, a memorable example of the meaning of free election in a democratic society.

CHAPTER 7

BALL

STANLEY MAILED US A GAY DISPATCH from Washington on the stationery of the people who put him up at their home over the Truman Inauguration:

Invited to Inaugural Ball, of course. Held Ticket 3,108. A very low number. Make no mistake about *that*. Feverish personal preparations before leaving for Ball. Cummerbund would not hook. Would *half* hook. Worse than not hooking at all. Comforted by thought that Tom Dewey reputed to own cummerbund that will not hook. Truman a waistcoat man. Has gone far. Got grip on myself about ten o'clock and hooked cummerbund. Into living room for one for the road. No liquor to be served at the Ball. Into big automobile with laughing crowd of friends. All Democrats. Nobody hiding fact under bushel basket. Ladies fetching in pink and gray satin tinged with silk and bits of mustard topped by lace dropping midway to sequined taffeta. Loved that one for the road. Men superb, composed, in white tie and tails. Mine only cummerbund in car. Sped toward National Guard

Armory, where Ball being held. Spied Armory blocks away. Rainbow of colored floodlights trained on building. Huge structure. Contents of car unloaded in front of long canopy, happy, laughing. Like a wedding. Felt young again. Ladies had trouble getting out of car. Too much dressing. Walked under canopy into Armory lobby, into throng of admirals, generals, short-order cooks, ministers plenipotentiary, Secret Service men, black ties, white ties, dignity, dignity, dignity. Handed gardenia flown to Washington from Mexico for the Inaugural Ball, courtesy American Airlines. Handed souvenir program with golden cover. Handed hat-and-coat check. Entire floor sanded for dancing. Looked like Miami Beach. Tremendous stage midway along one side of Armory, bandstand revolving. Guy Lombardo and orchestra revolving out of sight, Xavier Cugat and orchestra revolving into sight. Cugat on the beam. Bigger baton than Toscanini. Played rumbas. Hotcha! Spied Chief Justice Vinson observing proceedings with friendly judicial eye. Bowed to him. He bowed back. What a country! Handed another gardenia flown to Washington from Mexico for the Inaugural Ball, courtesy American Airlines. Handed bright-red rose. "Sorry, no more gardenias," said lady handing out roses. "Roses courtesy Roses, Inc." Handed lady my two gardenias. Cugat revolved out of sight, Benny Goodman revolved into sight. Goodman hot, very hot. Marine Band lined up before stage. President Truman and party, including Mrs. and Miss Truman, took box seats overlooking dance floor. President obviously happy. Why not?

Into balcony. Bowed to Secretary Forrestal, stepped aside for General Bradley, Indian-wrestled with Secretary Krug, and started toward President, to offer congratulations, but was told by Secret Service, gently, to go away. Went away. Back downstairs. Handed rose. Ate rose. Bowed to Chester Bowles, Tom Clark, Elmer Davis, Secretary Sullivan, and Secretary Snyder. Return bows from all. Free country. An hour of this. Hard core of dancers in middle of floor, shuffling mass of rubberneckers walking around edge of floor, gaping at folk in lower-level boxes. Stopped to pass time of day with Margaret O'Brien. Such a *little* girl. Tiny eyes set close together, pale complexion, neatly manicured nails. "You're up late," I said. She said nothing. Over to Shirley Temple, in box with Chief Justice Vinson. Got Shirley Temple autograph. Saw Jinx Falkenburg. Looks thinner than she sounds. Spied Margaret Truman, now in floor box. Walked over to offer congratulations, but was told by Secret Service, gently, to go away. Glanced up at President. Still in balcony box. Looked healthier than anybody else in Armory. Looked as though he wanted to dance with Bess. Scheme obviously nixed by Secret Service. Picked gardenia up from floor for lovely old lady in acres of lace. Said, "Shall we dance?" "Charmed," she said. While waltzing together was informed lady had danced at Benjamin Harrison Inaugural Ball. Waltzed, a stunning pair, under President's box. Had feeling President looked down enviously. Lady had next dance reserved for a Richmond Blue. Time to go home. Waited thirty-five minutes for hat and coat. In hatcheck line met fine gentleman from Lamar, Missouri. Said he knew Truman when Truman was a boy. Said he was fine boy.

January 1949

CHAPTER 8

MR. SECRETARY

By tradition, when the great doors of the House of Representatives open and the Cabinet enters to hear the President's State of the Union address, the first to enter is the Secretary of State, thus acknowledging the immense responsibility of the officer guiding foreign policy.

I had the good fortune of being a close friend of Dean Acheson's close friend Stanley Woodward, who had been Chief of Protocol under FDR and Truman, and Truman's Ambassador to Canada. This gave me remarkable access to the witty and brilliant Acheson. The night before the piece went to press, Mr. Ross came to my office. "Has the Secretary read the piece?" he asked. "No," I said. "I never send galley proofs." Mr. Ross looked grim. "For Christ sake, Hamburger," he said. "There's a cold war! Russia! Stuff!" I suggested calm should prevail. "Let's call the Secretary," I said, "and find out what he thinks." We reached Acheson at home. No, he did not wish to see proofs. He would prefer to read the Profile when it came out.

Dean Gooderham Acheson, the forty-ninth Secretary of State of the United States of America, has been engaged most of his life in a running battle with his appearance. He is an impressive example of the maxim that there is more to a man than meets the eye. What meets the eye that looks at Acheson is an austere, tall, slim, long-legged, and outrageously mustached fashion plate, a parody of the diplomatic virtues, with matching tie and handkerchief, brown leather dispatch case, and black Homburg. The discrepancy between the outer Acheson and the inner Acheson is huge. The inner Acheson is gregarious and warmhearted, possessed of a quick wit and a skeptical mind, impatient of procedural form, self-analytical to an advanced degree, and a taskmaster who will accept from himself nothing less than what he considers perfection. Often, shifting from foot to foot at an official function, Acheson is painfully conscious of the impression his appearance is making on strangers. Some perverse devil deep inside him compels him to play—for a time, at least—the role expected of him. Not long ago, at a particularly humid gathering of people who concern themselves with foreign affairs, the outer Acheson pulled noncommittally at his mustache, raised and lowered his thick eyebrows in a manner that could signify everything or nothing, engaged in talk so small as to be almost invisible, and bowed from the waist with punctilio. Not until a stranger in striped trousers approached him and said fatuously, "Mr. Acheson, you must be proud indeed of your achievements in life" did the outer Acheson send forth a hurry call for the inner Acheson. "Sir," replied the Secretary, dipping into his gag file, "all that I know I learned at my mother's knee, and other low joints."

The Secretary's remark was characteristic but inaccurate. His formal education was extensive and included attendance at such high joints as Groton, Yale, and the Harvard Law School. At Groton, he learned that people are expected to have a fervent juvenile loyalty to something about which they basically don't give a hoot, such as a freshman class or a baseball team. "At Groton, I didn't happen to feel like conforming," Acheson said recently, "and to my surprise and astonishment I discovered not only that an independent judgment might be the right one but that a man was actually alive and breathing once he had made it." At Yale, he learned that life can be fun. At Harvard, he learned that the human mind, though complicated, is probably the most effective instrument available for solving the problems of the human race. "This was a tremendous discovery—the discovery of the power of thought," Acheson says. "Not only did I become aware of this wonderful mechanism, the brain, but I became aware of an unlimited mass of material that was lying about the world waiting to be stuffed into the brain. It was just one step further to the philosophic approach to matters—to learning that you need not make up your mind in advance, that there is no set solution to a problem, and that decisions are the result of analyzing the facts, of tussling and grappling with them."

Acheson's informal education has been even more extensive, and certain aspects of it have been equally fruitful. When he graduated, fifth in his class, from the Harvard Law School, Felix Frankfurter, who was then teaching at Harvard, recommended him for the post of law clerk to the late Louis D. Brandeis, an Associate Justice of the Supreme Court. Acheson received the appointment and remained with Brandeis two years. They were years of hard, almost uninterrupted work. Justice Brandeis believed that the quality of a man's work was more important than the quantity, that there was something attainable beyond "best," and that anything less was not enough. A man of fiercely moral makeup and with an acute feeling for the larger problems of society, he sharpened these same things in Acheson. The association with Brandeis was not confined to the Justice's chambers, and a strong bond developed between the two men. "Throughout these years we brought him all our problems and all our troubles, and he had time for all of us," Acheson said when, two decades later, in 1941, he spoke at Brandeis's funeral. "In talk with him, the problems answered themselves. A question, a comment, and the difficulties began to disappear; the dross and shoddy began to appear for what it was. . . . I have heard him speak of some achievement of one of us with all the pride, and of some sorrow or disappointment of another with all the tenderness, of a father speaking of his sons. We are the generation which has lived during and between two wars. We have lived in the desert years of the human spirit. Years when the cry was 'What is truth?'. . . In a time of moral and intellectual anarchy and frustration, he handed on the great tradition in the mind and spirit of man."

Acheson's association with Brandeis led to friendships with other members of the Court, notably the late Oliver Wendell Holmes, who appears to have been a magnet to anyone who came anywhere near him. The influence of Holmes was of quite a different character. Whereas Brandeis exhibited certain of the forbidding qualities of an Old Testament prophet, Holmes was a caustic, aged, all-wise Grand Lama. In his wisdom there was a magical, twinkly leaven. Brandeis saw through to the heart of a matter after a painstaking sifting of the evidence, then reached his conclusion and stood four-square behind it. Holmes followed the same process, but having reached a clear conclusion he could, with equal sureness, demolish his own argument. Throughout his early years in Washington, Acheson paid monthly calls on Justice Holmes at his house. The Justice did most of the talking. "I felt that he had all knowledge in his head," Acheson says. "Of course, the old man relished his nuggets. He would hit on a rich, ripe phrase and repeat it over and over. He used to say and say again that man was created to form general principles and none of them was worth a damn."

Acheson's intellectual style is his own, but observers of his career feel that it happily shows the influence of both Brandeis and Holmes. As a practicing attorney in Washington on and off for twenty-eight years, he was further schooled in the value of objectivity in the face of facts. "Dean never let facts throw him," a former legal associate has said. "He always maintained a cool detachment. Some lawyers get so steamed up they think their client is the Lord God Almighty fifteen minutes after he has stepped into the office. Acheson always saw the client as representing a soluble problem, and little more." Some years ago, a prominent New York industrialist asked Acheson's firm— Covington, Burling, Rublee, Acheson & Shorb—to handle the appeal of a case that had been badly bungled in the lower courts. Acheson agreed to plead the case in a higher court, came to New York to talk over matters with the client, and that same day wrote a brief that was a model of conciseness, clarity, and persuasiveness. The client ordered several hundred copies printed on deckle-edge rag paper and planned to distribute them among his plant managers, executives, and salesmen. A couple of evenings later, he spied Acheson at a table in the Oak Room of the Hotel Plaza, nursing a nightcap and pulling abstractedly on his mustache. "Mr. Acheson," said the client, wringing his hand, "your brief is a work of art, a masterpiece of legal thinking." Acheson gave the man the long, gentle, tolerant look he reserves for persons whose enthusiasm gets the better of them. "Not a bad brief," he said slowly. "It almost convinced *me*."

Acheson's convictions are numerous and deep, but for the most part he naturally confines his official remarks as Secretary of State to clear expositions of established public policy. His speeches are an anomaly in Washington, since he writes most of them himself and they are in English that can be parsed. They are seldom indicative of anything beyond the outer Acheson, the lawyer-diplomat stating his case in formal terms. Of the North Atlantic Treaty, for example, he has said, "The treaty is the practical expression of the determination that an aggressor cannot divide these nations and pick them off one by one." Of the United Nations, "The future of America is closely related to the extension of democratic principles and practices in other areas; we believe the United Nations is the proper agency for promoting that extension by peaceful and proper means." Of the anticipated meeting in Paris of the Council of Foreign Ministers, in the spring of 1949, "I cannot . . . honestly state whether or not this new attempt will end in success. No one can tell. The answer will have to await the meeting." Once, however, in the summer of 1946, when he was Under-Secretary of State, Acheson revealed to a public gathering some of his more private thoughts. Invited to address the Associated Harvard Clubs in Boston, he accepted, with the intention of discussing in generalities some major problems facing the State Department. A few of the younger men in his office felt that there was no point in his making that kind of speech. "Dean," one of them said, "why not put down on paper what's really on your mind? To hell with the old-fashioned speech!" The Under-Secretary decided to take the suggestion. On two successive evenings, he sat at his desk in his study writing in longhand. He kept a Scotch highball at his elbow and sipped from it occasionally, the more readily to summon the inner Acheson. The result was a speech entitled "Random Harvest," which holds a high place among Achesoniana. As Brandeis and Holmes were in their day, Acheson is the center of an admiring and devoted group of young men, mostly lawyers with a Harvard background, and in this circle "Random Harvest" is favored reading. In it, his friends feel, the two Achesons merged and found a common expression. "If one is to spin from his own visceral wisdom," Acheson declared at one point, "he must say, first, 'I shall not be a fake,' and, second, 'What do I know, or think I know, from my own experience, and not by literary osmosis?' An honest answer would be, 'Not much; and I am not too sure of most of it.'. . . One thing, however, seems pretty sure—that the tasks which grow out of the relations of our country with other countries are hard ones. . . . For a long time we have gone along with some well-tested principles of conduct: That it was better to tell the truth than falsehoods; that a half-truth was no truth at all; that duties were older than and as fundamental as rights; that, as Justice Holmes put it, the mode by which the inevitable came to pass was effort; that to perpetrate a harm was always wrong, no matter how many joined in it, but to perpetrate it on a weaker person or people was particularly detestable. . . . Our institutions are founded on the assumption that most people follow these principles most of the time because they want to, and the institutions work pretty well when this assumption is true. . . . It seems to me the path of hope is toward the concrete, toward the manageable. . . . But it is a long and tough job and one for which we as a people are not particularly suited. We believe that any problem can be solved with a little ingenuity and without inconvenience to the folks at large. . . . And our name for problems is significant. We call them headaches. You take a powder and they are gone. These pains about which we have been talking are not like that. They are like the pain of earning a living. They will stay with us until death. We have got to understand that all our lives the danger, the uncertainty, the need for alertness, for effort, for discipline will be upon us.

This is new to us. It will be hard for us. But we are in for it, and the only real question is whether we shall know it soon enough."

The Secretary of State leaves his ivy-covered, white-doored redbrick house, on a quiet street in Georgetown, at approximately ten minutes to nine in the morning. In one hand, he carries his brown dispatch case. On his head there is a black or a gray Homburg. These cool mornings, he wears a trim, gray topcoat. His sartorial equipment stops just short of undue elegance. He is partial to gray or blue suits with white stripes, ties with commanding, colorful diagonals, highly polished shoes, and blue-and-white candy-striped shirts with stiff white collars. In the morning light, his big reddish-gray mustache is an object of remarkable distinction. It has a personality of its own, and people who have happened by and seen Acheson emerge in the morning have often experienced the disquieting illusion that two entities are on their way to work, the Secretary and the Secretary's mustache. "Honestly," a neighbor who goes to work at about the same time said recently, "some mornings the mustache appears to be a step or two ahead of the Secretary; other mornings it appears to be a step or two behind." There is a solid basis for this illusion. Acheson is enormously fond of his mustache. It is for him not only a major link with his past but a guide to his present and his future. As a public figure, Acheson without his mustache would be like Roosevelt without his smile or Churchill without his cigar, but the mustache is more than a convenient cartoonist's symbol. Acheson's father, the late Edward Campion Acheson, Episcopal Bishop of Connecticut, wore a mustache, too—a Guardsman's mustache, thick and imperious, with a disdainful droop. While still in college, young Dean cultivated a similar growth, partly in defiance of and partly out of respect for his father. Throughout his early years at the bar and his first years in government service, his mustache was large, unruly, and reasonably aggressive. It was a pushy mustache, but its very pushiness betrayed its owner's uncertainty. Not until Acheson had become Under-Secretary of State, in 1945, was the mustache somewhat reduced in size and tilt. Though it once seemed about to climb his cheeks, like a vine seeking the sunlight, it now is comparatively self-controlled and at peace with itself, quietly aware of its responsibilities. While still bushy, it is no longer impenetrable, and while still giving off gay hints of the unpredictable, it is the adornment of a man who has conquered not only himself but his mustache. Acheson uses no wax or artificial flattener on it. He engages a great deal in the art of thinking, and with some violence, and while doing so he unconsciously pulls on the mustache and this gives it a bristly, well-tailored appearance. Most mornings, when Acheson leaves his house, taking a sharp look up and down the street from his front door, moving briskly along his short brick walk, and almost leaping down a flight of stone steps to the street, he and his mustache are in perfect harmony. On mornings when the Secretary is disturbed by a problem, the mustache asserts its independence, once again giving the impression of being a separate entity.

The Secretary walks to work. On every morning that it isn't raining, he covers the distance—a matter of a mile and a half—in the company of Justice Frankfurter, who is now one of his closest friends. Some mornings, Frankfurter, a short, bouncy man, picks Acheson up in front of the Secretary's house (they live three blocks and a half apart); on other mornings they meet at an agreed-upon spot. Conversation, on a variety of topics, is the mainstay of their walks. Frankfurter is one of the celebrated conversationalists of our day, and, whether he is standing or sitting, his talk covers a staggering range of subjects. Acheson himself is no slouch at conversation, but it's possible that he is at a slight disadvantage when on foot. Both men jealously guard the contents of their talks. "I'll tell you one thing," Justice Frankfurter said a while back to an inquiring acquaintance. "We never talk about the government or foreign policy. We just talk." Heading down a tree-lined street of Georgetown, they would be an artist's delight—the small, compact Justice taking two or three steps for every seven-league one of the tall, rangy Secretary, and both engrossed in conversation. On overcast mornings, the Justice's car creeps along behind. If it starts to rain, the two men hop in and the driver proceeds to the Department of State. The Department, which used to be in the antique, fricasseed structure across the street from the White House, on Pennsylvania Avenue, is now housed in a seven-story building that was constructed just before the last war for the War Department, which later moved to the Pentagon Building. It is in a section of Washington locally called Foggy Bottom, a term that refers not to the State Department or its policies but to the fact that it is a low area near the Potomac and often foggy.

About nine-fifteen on a good morning, the Secretary and the Justice, still talking, round a corner of the State Department Building. They walk together as far as the front steps. Acheson says goodbye to Frankfurter and starts up the steps. On four out of five mornings, Frankfurter has one final morsel of conversation, and he calls after Acheson, who pauses to listen and then goes into the building. Frankfurter's car then picks him up and takes him to the Supreme Court Building. Acheson enters his official world through a dark lobby, with square marble pillars, reminiscent of Egypt and of Hollywood, and takes a private elevator to his office, on the fifth floor. He steps from the elevator into a paneled waiting room containing some chairs and sofas upholstered in blue leather and several small mahogany tables. When he became Secretary of State, the walls of the antechamber were hung with colored reproductions of modern American paintings, including a Fiene, a Hurd, a Zorach, a Levi, and a Marsh. Mrs. Acheson, herself a painter, felt that the room should have something different, and she borrowed several lively primitive prints from the National Gallery as replacements. These include one of Old Rough-and-Ready Taylor on his horse. She also borrowed some scenes of the Mexican War, but out of diplomatic discretion the Secretary saw to it that they weren't hung. Acheson enters his office from the antechamber through a dark wood door. He is still staggered by the size of his office. Not long ago, he said of it, "I always have the feeling that I am walking into the cabin-class dining saloon on one of those old North German Lloyd liners." It is of Mussolini-type proportions, with a huge refectory table at one end, beneath a large oil of former Secretary of State Henry L. Stimson. The Secretary's desk, a massive mahogany object installed in Secretary Marshall's day, is midway along the windowed side of the room. His chair is high-backed and upholstered in red leather. At one side of his desk is an unabridged dictionary, at the other a globe of the world illuminated from within.

This is also a holdover from the tenure of Secretary Marshall. Against the wall opposite is a tremendous grandfather's clock. High above the clock, almost at the ceiling, are two dark paintings, which Mrs. Acheson borrowed from the Smithsonian Institution, one of the signing of the Treaty of Ghent and the other, painted by Mrs. Acheson's grandfather, John Mix Stanley, of the signing of a treaty with the Cherokee Indians. In a corner of the room is a group of comfortable red leather chairs, a sofa, and a coffee table. On the table are generally a dozen books of paper matches bearing the seal of the Department of State.

Acheson has a personal office force of two assistants—Lucius Battle, a young lawyer, and Miss Barbara Evans, who has been shuttling with Acheson between his law office and the Department of State for years—and three stenographers. Once Acheson has deposited his Homburg and topcoat in a closet and has sat down at his desk, either Battle or Miss Evans brings him the Logbook, a black leather-bound loose-leaf volume with "Top Secret" in silver across its cover. In the Logbook have been placed copies of the most important cables (to and from State Department offices in all parts of the world) of the last twelve hours. These have been carefully winnowed out by the Communications Room, the twenty-four-hour-a-day nerve center of the Department. Within a few minutes, the Secretary can bring himself up to date on the latest developments in the more critical problems facing the Department. Under each cable is a note or two of pertinent information. Acheson studies them until nine-thirty, and sometimes, following a practice that goes back to his early days in law, jots down salient points in longhand on sheets of yellow foolscap. Then, unless, of course, hell has broken loose somewhere in the world during the night, he holds a conference with Under-Secretary of State James Webb, Battle, and Carlisle Humelsine, the Director of the Executive Secretariat. Humelsine is the traffic policeman in charge of all the messages flowing in and out of the offices of the Secretary and the Under-Secretary. His office is halfway down a lengthy corridor that begins at Acheson's office and ends at Webb's, a chamber as vast as the Secretary's. These meetings generally last half an hour. During them,

Acheson discusses the new cables and plans his day's work. From ten o'clock on, his day is more or less flexible. He may start out by meeting with a group of Departmental experts to discuss important business. In conference, he follows a well-established pattern. Leaning far back in his red leather chair, taking notes in pencil, he listens to each man's exposition of his conception of the problem and his suggested remedy. Occasionally, Acheson asks a question, but he rarely expresses an opinion until everyone else in the room has had his say. He then summarizes what he has heard, points out the conflicts between the several points of view, attempts to reconcile them, and finally offers a solution based on the other men's opinions and his own. "His summations are much on the order of those of a fine judge charging a jury," a State Department official recently said. "He weighs, balances, thinks, and then gives his orders." Acheson may hold four or five such meetings during a morning, and meet briefly with foreign diplomats or other visiting dignitaries as well. In his encounters with foreign representatives, he is almost invariably good-humored, sympathetic, brief, and cryptic. Lord Halifax, the British Ambassador to the United States during the war, saw a lot of Acheson at that time. Halifax, a master of diplomatic nuance himself, once remarked to a friend that he envied Acheson's skill in that field. "I would be halfway back to the Embassy, still chuckling over some remark of his, before I realized that he hadn't told me a single, blessed thing," Halifax said.

Acheson is aware that a large number of visiting foreigners are eager to have a conversation with him, however short, to enhance their prestige back home. He obliges as far as he can, making the interviews as short as possible. Not long ago, a politician who had held high office in a Western European country and was attempting a comeback asked for an appointment to see the Secretary. "I really didn't have the time," Acheson told an acquaintance, "but I knew that this fellow would be crushed if he couldn't cable back home that he had stepped across the threshold of the Secretary of State's office. He had nothing to say, I had nothing to say, but he badly needed the cachet of having been in the office of the Secretary of State. He was very friendly to us during the war, so I had him in. He entered ceremoniously, bowed ceremoniously, shook hands ceremoniously, and

said, 'Mr. Secretary, what of the future?' 'What of it?' I said, and the
man shook hands and left. He had achieved what he wanted, and I
had lost, at the most, forty-five seconds."

On Wednesdays, at eleven, the Secretary holds his weekly press conferences in the State Department auditorium, three floors below his
office. Usually a hundred or more newspaper men turn up. Acheson's
conference rank high in attendance and popularity as Washington
press conferences go. Their popularity is indicative of the importance
of foreign affairs in America today, but Acheson is more than a little
responsible himself, because he brings his wit into fairly steady play
during the sessions. Wit is in short supply among high government
officials. There is a good deal of unconscious humor and an over-
abundance of horseplay of the hotfoot and dribble-glass variety, but
little wit. From time to time, however the shock of hearing a Secretary
of State operate with the light touch is more than some of the old press
hands can take, and Acheson guards himself against being too funny.
Lately there have been complaints that he is also guarding himself
against saying yes or no and has been falling into the Washington
habit of talking around a question.

Acheson prepares himself assiduously for his press conferences.
Every Tuesday night, he takes home a portfolio of reports and memo-
randa on topics that he and his aides think may be asked about by the
journalists in the morning. For several hours before he goes to bed, he
studies these and sketches out his answers. The consequence is that he
is rarely presented with a question he is not prepared to answer. In a
single conference, he may be called upon to discuss Ruhr policy, the
ex-Italian colonies, the Egyptian ruling house, Indonesia. China, Tito,
the extension of the lease on the United States Air Force base at
Dhahran, an obscure section of the United Nations Charter, the
atomic bomb, the financial condition of the United Kingdom, and several score other topics, the consideration of any one of which would
have been considered a half week's work by a Secretary of State a
quarter of a century ago. Acheson is ruefully amused by the eagerness
of the press. "One of the happy things about this conference," he said
one Wednesday, "is that I learned what it was about over the radio

before leaving the house. That seemed to me to be a triumph of modern journalism." On another occasion, he told the assembled group, "There is a certain dilemma between the great need for as full and as quick public information as possible and the equally great need for a certain amount of privacy and calm in reaching a formulation of the matter which you are going to discuss publicly." He is adroit at ducking a question he doesn't want to answer. Asked for detailed information on the postwar allocation of steel to Germany, he replied, "You have now gone over the narrow edge of my knowledge." Occasionally, to avoid answering, he will fall back on reminiscence. "I'll tell you a story," he said one morning in response to a query about something still secret. "My old law partner Judge Covington once went to an oyster roast down on the Eastern Shore of Maryland and had a fine time eating those wonderful oysters, until he was handed a red-hot one. Why, that oyster must have been two hundred and seventy degrees Fahrenheit. Old Judge Covington took one look at the oyster and said, 'A man would have to be a damn fool to swallow *that* one.'" "Thank you, Mr. Secretary," said a voice from the rear of the room, and the conference was over.

Fridays, at ten, the Secretary attends Cabinet meetings at the White House; every other Thursday afternoon, he attends a session of the National Security Council, a group consisting of the President, the Vice-President, the Secretary of State, the Secretary of Defense, the three Service Secretaries, and the head of the National Resources Planning Board. Mondays and Thursdays, at twelve-thirty, he goes over to the White House to talk with the President. He may see the President two or three times more every week, and he talks with him frequently on the phone. Like the other Cabinet officers, Acheson has a white telephone on his desk that is connected by direct wire to the White House. The relations between Acheson and Truman are among the happiest in Truman's official family. Cynical observers have said that Truman admires Acheson because he looks the way the President thinks a Secretary of State *should* look. "If Harry were a painter, and had never laid eyes on Acheson, and sat down to paint a picture of a foreign minister, he would come up with a life-size oil of Dean," a Republican congressman once remarked. Seated in the President's oval office threshing out questions that would stagger the gods, the President and his Secretary of State hit it off in a curiously old-fashioned comfortable, confident manner. Superficially different, the two men have startlingly similar aspects. Both come from small towns —Truman from Independence, Missouri, Acheson from Middletown, Connecticut—and both have roots in a relatively carefree and easy-going America. Politically and economically, both are to the left of what is customarily known as center but are lodged there in a conservative way. Both have a highly developed sense of loyalty. When Acheson appeared before the Senate Committee on Foreign Relations during the hearings on his nomination for Secretary of State, he spoke of his concept of the job. "The policies which President Truman has followed since he took office have been evolved with the help of two Secretaries of State," he said. "I served under both of them as their Under-Secretary. I think I know something of the circumstances and the problems which the President's actions were designed to meet. I think I know something of the need in American foreign policy for steadiness and continuity. During these years and the four years preceding . . . I think . . . I learned something about the function of an adviser to his chief—that that function was to be frank and forthright and vigorous in counsel, that it was to be energetic and loyal in accepting decisions and carrying them out."

"I would imagine," said Senator Tydings, "that there is also the inference that when any situation came up that you felt you could no longer adhere to, you would no longer be a member of the President's family."

"I anticipate nothing as unhappy as that, sir," replied Acheson, "but should it arise, of course your answer would be the only answer that an honorable man could give."

For his part, President Truman undoubtedly remembers that when he returned to Washington from Independence in November 1946, after the Democratic Party had taken a severe beating in the congressional elections, Acheson was the only high government official on hand to meet him at Union Station.

Acheson carries to his meetings with the President what he calls his Briefing Book, a loose-leaf volume of summaries of problems he wishes to discuss. He is never didactic or dramatic with the President, and asks him to question any ambiguous passages in his presentation. "Acheson never pushes a policy with Truman," a State Department official said a few weeks ago. "Rather, the two of them appear to evolve a policy working as a team. Of course, Acheson skillfully plants a seed here and a seed there but he never marks them as his own and he wants no credit for them." From all reports, President Truman is delighted with the working methods of his Secretary of State. Secretary Byrnes is said to have proceeded somewhat arbitrarily rather than by the patient, detailed, step-by-step method toward which Acheson is disposed. The President was so awed by Secretary Marshall that the relationship was never an entirely natural, relaxed one. Truman has perhaps more respect for Marshall than for any other living man—a feeling shared by Acheson—and this very fact made it impossible for the President to establish a give-and-take relationship with him. The President is unstinting in his praise of Acheson. "He's doing a whale of a job," he told a recent visitor at his office. "One of the finest men in government, and the results are already showing. I never wanted him to leave government service in the first place, but as I've said many times, you need an elephant hide and a barrel of money to stay." "A great chief," Acheson frequently murmurs to his aides in the State Department after a call at the White House.

On Mondays, the Secretary has lunch with the rest of the Cabinet at the White House. Other days, he lunches across the corridor from his office, in a small, upper-echelon dining room containing a half dozen or so tables and pallid etchings of several of our Embassies. Ordinarily, he goes into the dining room by himself and sits down with two or three other top officials wherever he finds an empty chair. The conversation is mostly confined to State Department business. Acheson generally eats a light lunch and returns to his office for sessions with a steady stream of Department officers. He holds many telephone conversations with senators and representatives, sometimes about vital business, sometimes about nothing more pressing than a request for a letter of introduction to the ambassador of some country a friend of a congressman intends to visit. The Secretary is on chummy terms with a host of congressmen, partly because he was once Assistant Secretary of State in charge of liaison with Congress. Much to the surprise of many of his friends, he got along famously with the senators and representatives; he not only had a great affection for various members of Congress but had as many rambling jokes stored away in his head as Vice-President Barkley. He took a liking to meeting with Leslie Biffle, the Secretary of the Senate, and Biffle's cronies in Biffle's office in the Capitol, where bourbon and branch water are consumed in moderate, *gemütlich* quantities and state business is discussed in an atmosphere of anecdote and knee-slapping.

Of necessity, Acheson devotes considerable time to Congressional relations. When the State Department is advocating a piece of legislation, he may spend as much time on Capitol Hill as in his office, appearing in executive session before a Congressional committee or at an open hearing in one of the large, marble-pillared rooms in the Senate or House Office Building. Open hearings have the atmosphere of a bullfight, with the Secretary as the bull. The bull usually emerges from the fight unscathed. The sessions ordinarily begin with the Secretary's reading a prepared statement in a dull, bored, nasal voice. Acheson is not at ease with prepared statements; they cramp his style. He comes into his own during the question-and-answer period. He has often sat for two or three hours under steady questioning, for several days running, without losing his poise or his air of deep concern with every question. He will repeat phrases like "You are entirely correct, sir," or "I cannot see how the position could be better expressed," or "I am glad you brought that matter up, Senator," with such conviction that sometimes, before the question period is over, the members of Congress are pleading the proposition Acheson has set out to prove.

Acheson tries to finish each working day by being alone in his office. "It's humanly impossible to handle all the problems that come across this desk in a day," he told a caller a few weeks ago. "I try to delegate as much authority as possible and leave myself toward evening with just a little time to think. There are usually half a dozen crises on hand before supper, you know." The Secretary's late-afternoon thinking is frequently interrupted by the flow of paperwork. All day, Mr.

Humelsine, down the corridor, has been gathering papers for the Secretary's signature. He has devised a method whereby Acheson does not lose much time in scanning them. Every paper to be signed reaches the Secretary's desk clipped to a batch of other papers pertinent to the matter involved. He can simply read the first page of the attached batch, which summarizes the facts and presents the recommendation of the Department, or, if he has doubts about the problem, refer to the attached file. A small green oblong blotter bearing the word "SIGN" in black letters is clipped to the paper to be signed over the point where Acheson's signature is to be placed. At six-thirty sharp, in a garage in the basement, Rudolph, the official chauffeur of the Secretary of State, tunes up the Secretary's official black Cadillac. Upstairs, sometime between six-thirty and six-forty-five, having walked approximately a quarter of a mile up and down his office in deep thought, and having stopped at his desk to sign twenty or thirty papers, Acheson crams a challenging bunch of documents into his dispatch case, puts on his Homburg and coat, descends in his private elevator to the basement, gets into his car, and goes home for supper.

Few things delight Acheson quite so much as reminiscing about his childhood. The more complicated his official life becomes, the more pleasure he derives from taking a rare few moments off to recall, wistfully and sometimes perhaps romantically, certain aspects of his early days. Once he gets going on the life of a small boy in Middletown, Connecticut, at the beginning of the century (i.e., himself), only pressing problems of state can divert him. Early last spring, during a brief lull in the delicate negotiations for the lifting of the Berlin blockade, the Secretary sat down in his office with a reporter to talk over the old times. As Acheson spoke, the pressures of his high post seemed to lessen. Features that are normally forbidding—his bristly reddish-gray mustache, his penetrating, almost popping eyes—became youthfully and gently mischievous. Crossing and uncrossing his legs, the Secretary painted an idyll of boyhood in which every lad on every block was a Tom Sawyer, every day was filled with explosively carefree adventure, and there was chicken every Sunday. Suddenly, the door swung open, and an aide looked in. The Secretary waved him back and said, "Just a couple of minutes more, please." He continued for a couple of minutes to spin his tales of pony rides and Wild West shows, of sandlot ball games and hitches on ice wagons, until, once again, the aide interrupted. "I must see you for a few minutes, sir," he pleaded. His arms were filled with papers. Acheson got up and turned to his visitor with a shrug and a sigh. As the reporter left, he noticed that the Secretary's mustache, a moment before as impish as a false mustache attached by a piece of wax to the face of a small boy, was stiff and commanding.

Dean Acheson was born with at least a silver-plated spoon in his mouth. His father, Edward Campion Acheson, an Englishman of Scotch-Irish descent, emigrated in 1881 from England to Canada, studied for the Anglican ministry at the University of Toronto, received his theological degree, and came to New York as assistant rector of St. George's Church. Soon thereafter he married Eleanor Gertrude Gooderham, a member of a wealthy Canadian distilling family, and moved to Middletown, a town of twenty thousand, thirty miles north of New Haven, on the Connecticut River, where he became rector of Holy Trinity Church. The Achesons settled down in a large, roomy brick house on an elm-lined street, where two sons and a daughter were born to them. Acheson's father, who became Episcopal Bishop of Connecticut in 1915, was tall and imposing, had decided views on a variety of topics, from child-raising to the need for improving conditions in factories, and in the house often wore a blue jacket with bright silver buttons. Shortly after Dean was born, on April 11, 1893, a neighborhood couple brought two of their sons, in their teens, to call one evening. "Fine boys you have there," said the rector. "Where do they go to school?" He was told that they attended a new academy called Groton, and that they were receiving what appeared to be a sound, classical, and disciplined education. "I have a new son upstairs," said the rector. "We'll enter him in Groton." "And that's how I went to Groton some fourteen years later," Acheson recalled not long ago. "Father's method was direct—a simple question asked and a decision reached."

For the first few years, his elementary education was put in the hands of a governess, but he persistently managed to elude her with admirable ingenuity and light out in his pony cart. In those days, the Secretary says, a child didn't have many serious problems. "Today, Heaven help them, children face nothing but problems," he says. "They can't do this, they can't do that. They dare not go into the street, for fear of being run over; they must not stay in the house, for fear of becoming sheltered. Our pleasures in Middletown were of the simplest, most beautiful kind. The high spots of each day came after supper, at twilight. There were two major events. One followed immediately after the other. First, all the boys and girls raced down to the firehouse, where every evening the shining wagon and the well-brushed horses were brought onto the street. Firemen slid down poles. The horses and wagon were put back in the firehouse. That was all, but, oh, what pleasure! With perhaps sixty seconds to cover the distance, everybody then raced to the wharf to watch the arrival of the Hartford boat. She stayed only a couple of minutes, picking up passengers, and started downriver toward the Sound, on her way to New York. To me, it seemed that the ladies and gentlemen promenading the deck of that ship were the most fortunate people on earth, and watching them, night after night, I imagined myself plowing across the open sea, some nights to Europe, some nights to China, some nights to darkest Africa. But the moment the boat disappeared, I was happy to be still in Middletown—there were so many things to do."

The comings and goings of the Hartford boat were young Acheson's only contact with the world beyond Middletown, except for occasional excursions to New Haven with his father. "From the time of my first trip to New Haven, Yale was the college I wanted to attend," Acheson says. "This was, in a sense, strange, since Wesleyan is in Middletown, and one of the juicy thrills of my boyhood was to make for the Wesleyan ball field and hang around the outfield for an hour or so during batting practice. Sometimes, if you hung around long enough, a fly ball might come your way and you were allowed to catch it and toss it back to some big boy with a 'W' on his sweater, who would sometimes actually say, 'Thanks, kid.' A rather impressive moment." Problems of foreign policy rarely intruded upon the Middletown cosmos. "The only foreign-policy problems I remember," Acheson says, "were created by Father, who would always hang out the British flag on Queen Victoria's birthday, enraging the Irish, and the Irish flag on St. Patrick's Day, scandalizing the so-called proper elements. When the Boer War came along, Father chose to side with the British, and this made the Irish quite sore. They were never sure where he stood—nor was anybody else, for that matter. But really, as far as problems beyond our shores went, why should anyone have been bothered by them? The pattern of one's life in Middletown had an ordered regularity. Life flowed easily and pretty democratically. Take Mr. Bostick. Poor Mr. Bostick! Everybody was upset about *that*. It shows how much people cared in those days. Mr. Bostick was a conductor for the New Haven Railroad, on the Saybrook-Hartford run. He was also in overnight charge of the train and was supposed to see it safely parked on a siding in Middletown. But by the time Mr. Bostick got to Middletown each evening, he would be famished. He'd leave the train out on the main track and go home for supper, and a brakeman would come along later and roll it onto a siding. One night the train went off the track, or rolled off the track, or something, and Bostick was docked thirty days for not having attended to his duties. Most of Middletown was incensed and felt it was a dreadful punishment and quite unjust."

Acheson's easygoing life came to an end when he went to Groton. He had been sent to Hamlet Lodge, a less lofty boarding school at Pomfret, when he was nine, but for only a short period. "The first thing I noticed at Groton was the seriousness with which teams were chosen and the sudden and arbitrary loyalties one was expected to entertain," he says. "Back in Middletown, if you wanted a ball game, you went out to a lot and found some other fellows and chose up sides. The games went merrily along until someone got into a fight or was called for dinner. At Groton, it was a more intense procedure." In 1911, outfitted with a splendid wardrobe and a fairly large allowance, Acheson went to Yale. He was only a passable scholar there, but he was a rousing success at the art of living. His classmates remember him chiefly for his dazzling wardrobe and his quick tongue. "Dean moved in a fast circle and seemed to have a great deal more money than he actually had," a former classmate recalled recently. "He was never what you could honestly call gay—just as he isn't today—but he was refreshingly bright, and intent upon enjoying himself. He shunned the abstractions, for example, and kept far from the literary life on the campus, or anything that might have smacked of culture with a capital 'C.'" Acheson rowed on the freshman crew but was too light to make the varsity. He joined a number of clubs, including the Turtles, the Hogans, the Mohicans, and the Grill Room Grizzlies. Mostly, the members met to talk, sing songs, and tell rather poor jokes. More important, Acheson was tapped for one of the Yale secret societies, Scroll and Key, a big tap in the Yale world.

After graduating from Yale in 1915, Acheson went on to Harvard Law School, where he roomed for a year with Cole Porter. Acheson was immensely stimulated by Harvard. He discovered that he possessed a mind and that, applied to legal problems, it functioned with ease and swiftness. In 1917, while still at Harvard, he married Miss Alice Stanley, the daughter of a Detroit railroad lawyer; she had been a roommate of his sister's at Wellesley. Soon after that, the United States having entered the First World War, Acheson signed up with the Navy as an ensign in an overseas-transportation unit. He was stationed in the Brooklyn Navy Yard and never got overseas. After the war, he went back to Harvard, received his degree, and was recommended by one of his law professors, Felix Frankfurter, for the post of law clerk to Louis D. Brandeis, an Associate Justice of the Supreme Court.

Acheson served two fruitful years under Brandeis, and then was invited to join a new Washington law firm, Covington, Burling & Rublee. Today, the firm, which later expanded into Covington, Burling, Rublee, Acheson & Shorb, and since Acheson became Secretary has been Covington, Burling, Rublee, O'Brian & Shorb, is among the most successful in the country. One of the original partners, Edward Burling, a tall, thin, agile, sardonic-looking septuagenarian who bears a resemblance to the fictional Mr. Tutt, is still active in the firm. According to his associates, Burling has a mind that can clearly see eight sides of every question. He has always surrounded himself professionally with young men who not only know law but give him intellectual pleasure. Impressed by young Acheson, he put him to work, as a starter, on an important case, a matter involving a number of neutral Norwegian ships that had been seized by the United States government during the war. Covington, Burling & Rublee represented the Norwegian government. The controversy was over the amount of reparations the United States owed Norway. The United States felt it owed no more than three million dollars; Norway felt she should get eighteen. Acheson spent a year digging into the law, went to Oslo in 1922, with Burling, and soon afterward pleaded his first case in any courtroom before the old Permanent Court of Arbitration, at The Hague. He was toweringly arrogant. On the opening day of the trial, mounting the staircase to the small box where pleading lawyers stood, he told the Court that the attorney for the United States government had, a few moments before, insulted his client, the Royal Norwegian government. He demanded an apology.

"Do you mean to say that you are demanding an apology from your own government?" asked one of the five presiding judges.

"I am, sir," said Acheson. Burling, who was sitting in the courtroom, experienced a sensation of dizziness. He hurriedly scribbled a note, and handed it to an attendant.

"From your own government?" repeated the judge.

"Indeed, sir," said Acheson. At that moment, the note reached him. He opened it ceremoniously, read "For God's sake, come down fast," and went down the staircase, with aplomb. Mr. Burling mildly suggested a bit more caution, and Acheson remounted the stairs. He achieved a highly satisfactory settlement of twelve million dollars for Norway.

Back in Washington, Acheson settled into the traditional routine of a successful lawyer in a successful firm. He bought the house he still lives in, near the corner of Twenty-eighth and P Streets, in Georgetown, and enlarged it. The Achesons now have three grown children, as well as two grandchildren. Jane, their oldest child, is married to Dudley Brown, who is vice-president of the Milwaukee Gas & Light Co. David, a lawyer, works with the Atomic Energy Commission. Mary, the youngest, is married to William Bundy, who is associated with Acheson's old law firm. In the late twenties, the Achesons bought a piece of land near Sandy Springs, Maryland, on which there was a rundown farmhouse built in 1795 as a tobacco barn, and set about remodeling it. Acheson is an incorrigible amateur architect and has often told friends that he feels he missed his vocation. The Achesons turned the house into a weekend place, a cozy maze of book-filled rooms and hooked rugs. During the twenties and thirties, Acheson kept horses and cattle. He rode strenuously and taught his children to ride. "The riding lessons were supposed to be taken quite seriously," his younger daughter said not long ago. "Father insisted that we have the proper form on a horse, and no excuses."

Given complete freedom of professional choice, Acheson would unquestionably have patterned his legal career after that of the English barrister, who pleads cases before the courts but has no direct contact with the people whose cases he is pleading. Clients often bored and distressed Acheson. He did not feel any obligation to comfort or sympathize with them. Some of them, desiring a combination legal adviser and family doctor, felt that he was too disinterested. In 1926, when he was thirty-three, he was made a partner in the firm. For years, although he was not even slightly charmed by the work, he handled a great many tax problems. Acheson's reputation, however, was made as an appellate lawyer for complicated cases. "Once you have acquired a reputation as a noted appellate lawyer, you get cases with a hopelessly sour posture," a prominent attorney has remarked. "Once one of our kind gets into the mists and convolutions of appellate work, he is doing splendidly, we like to think, if he emerges victorious in ten percent of his cases." Acheson won around twenty percent of his cases before the United States Supreme Court. A lost case often brought him as much kudos as a victory, lawyers being as sensitive to the skill of a jouster as to the decisions he wins. In 1931, in a case that gave him considerable renown, Acheson represented the State of Arizona in a suit against the States of California, Nevada, Utah, New Mexico, Colorado, and Wyoming. Arizona wanted to retain what she thought was her just share of the water of the Colorado River for irrigation. That share, she claimed, was threat-

ened by the building of Boulder Dam, a project to which the other
states, under an act of Congress, were parties. At one point in his argument, Acheson offered to prove that the Colorado River was not navigable and hence the federal government had no jurisdiction over it.
The Colorado River, he said, was a wild, turbulent stream. It had deep
gorges, rapids, falls, treacherous curves, and other deathtraps. It was
beautiful—one of nature's incomparable pearls—but not navigable.
The Supreme Court thought otherwise. Justice Brandeis, who was
like a father to Acheson, delivered the blow. Records had revealed to
the Court that ten or twelve voyagers had navigated enough of the
river to render it legally navigable. Among them was one unsung hobo
on a raft.

In 1933, when Franklin D. Roosevelt became President, one of
Acheson's close friends, Lewis Douglas, of Arizona (it was Douglas
who had wanted Acheson to take on the Arizona case), urged the
President to appoint Acheson Solicitor General. The President had
someone else in mind for that post, but he made Acheson Under-
Secretary of the Treasury. Acheson was forty. The Secretary of the
Treasury, William H. Woodin, was ill most of the time he held office,
and a large portion of his work was turned over to Acheson. Acheson
was spiritually inclined toward the New Deal, but temperamentally
he was never entirely at home in the theatrical hurly-burly of its early
days. Plans to improve man's lot on earth appealed to him enormously, but, being a lawyer, he occasionally felt the need for a few
hours to think matters over. He was a vast admirer of the President,
and was stunned by the scope of Roosevelt's interests and the ease
with which he could shift his attention from one large project to
another. Early in the New Deal era, Acheson went to the White House
with a group of other government people to see the President. The
door to his study was open. Seated at his desk was Roosevelt, surrounded by a milling group of advisers. In his mouth was his long
cigarette holder, cocked at the customary angle. Someone thrust a
paper at him. He read it rapidly and signed it, listened briefly to two
or three of his advisers, smiled, jotted down some notes, answered

the telephone, signed some more papers, whispered to a man at his elbow, and, glancing toward the door, spied the waiting group outside. "Come on in!" cried the President. "We're doing a land-office business!"

Acheson parted company with the administration less than six months after he had become Under-Secretary. The President, in his desire to hoist prices from their disastrous depression level, got the notion that he should fiddle with the price of gold. Acheson demurred. The government, he claimed, lacked the right. The President is said to have replied, impatiently, that he was interested in finding a method of accomplishing what he had in mind, not in being told that the scheme was impossible. Stanley Reed, now an Associate Justice of the Supreme Court and then counsel for the Reconstruction Finance Corporation, upheld a plan by which the government would raise the price of gold, and thus devaluate the dollar, by buying gold with discounted Reconstruction Finance Corporation short-term obligations. Once again, Acheson demurred. "Those were trying days for Dean," one of his old friends, a distinguished legal scholar, recently said. "He had run head-on into the great moral dilemma of our age: At what point can undesirable means be justified by a socially desirable goal? In other words, when do you, in all conscience and pondering the imponderables, break the eggs to make the omelet?" Quite a few of Acheson's well-to-do friends considered the scheme simply a scatter-brained fantasy, likely to destroy their hearths and homes. Although displeased with their point of view, Acheson found himself, for an entirely different set of reasons, on their side. He took the problem to his friend Brandeis, who fortified his former law clerk's resistance to the proposal. Acheson sent the President a memorandum expressing his objections to the Reed plan. "Quite clearly," he wrote, "it would not be a discount justifiable for revenue purposes . . . to consider it as a discount at all within the meaning of that term as used by legislators would be to open wide the door for any and every kind of manipulation for ulterior purposes." Would Mr. Acheson be willing to accept an opinion from the Attorney General, the President asked the Treasury Department. Of course, replied Acheson. He added that he was also willing to resign. Before any opinion was presented, the President announced Acheson's resignation to a group of newspapermen, some of whom, in turn, mentioned it to Acheson, who had not been informed but was not entirely surprised. His code does not permit him to show distress, shock, or disappointment, and when his successor, Henry Morgenthau, Jr., took the oath of office, he was on hand, cool, genial, and in complete control of his mustache. The President, a man with an acute appreciation of gallantry, watched Acheson throughout the ceremony. When it was over, he said, "Dean, you're a sport!"

Feeling none too sporty, Acheson returned to his law firm. He had more clients than he could handle, and he prospered, but he was not a contented man. "Something came over Dean," a former partner said a while ago. "At some point along the road, he lost a measure of his self-confidence. He began to ask himself questions—where he was going, by what route, for what reason—and this was a new and strange experience." One thing that bothered Acheson was his attitude toward the practice of law. What had originally appealed to him was the excitement of the pursuit, through a labyrinth of circumstances, of a logical solution to a problem, but now this pursuit was only mildly exciting. "Dean took pleasure in finding the answers to riddles," the former partner said. "The nature of the riddles did not concern him. He was not a man to wander into the penumbra of thought." Acheson practiced law through the rest of the thirties, but he also kept up an interest in public affairs. He had enjoyed government service.

Acheson supported Roosevelt in 1936 and again in 1940. He was deeply concerned about the rise of Hitlerism, and he became an influential member of the Committee to Defend America by Aiding the Allies. "We must focus the full power of America," he told the fortieth-anniversary convention of the International Ladies' Garment Workers' Union, in 1940, "first, to produce the materials with which the free peoples of Europe may fight; second, to prepare ourselves to fight; and, finally, to harden and discipline our wills so that if and when the moment comes we shall not be defeated by irresolution or doubt." Acheson felt that the survival of one free nation was bound up with the survival of all free nations. It was inconceivable to him that the

United States should watch Great Britain go down without making every effort to save her. In August of that year, along with Charles C. Burlingham, Thomas D. Thacher, and George Rublee, Acheson signed a lengthy and now historic letter to *The New York Times,* setting forth, in involved legal language, the proposition that old United States destroyers could legally be exchanged for British bases without congressional sanction. The letter, which was composed by Acheson, created a furor in Washington. "Dean, when he made up his mind about the destroyer deal, once again faced the great moral dilemma," the legal scholar who commented upon his attitude toward the gold problem said in the same conversation. "The free world had to be saved. Those old destroyers would help to save it. Dean is a resilient man, and here was a case in which the eggs, in all conscience, could be broken—indeed, *had* to be broken."

In February, 1941, Acheson was appointed Assistant Secretary of State by Roosevelt. He held office in the State Department for six and a half years—through the days just before this country got into the war, through the war itself, and through the disillusioning period that immediately followed it. He served as Assistant Secretary under Hull and Stettinius and as Under-Secretary under Byrnes and Marshall. In those years, he mastered the workings of the Department of State and mastered himself as well. When he entered the Department, his mustache was a good quarter inch longer at each end than it was when he resigned, in the summer of 1947. Its diminution was almost imperceptible—a slow, gradual change, signifying his increasing self-confidence. He was then known in Washington as the "Number One Number Two Man," a term he did not relish. His assignments were of the kind that could be called big and hot potatoes. Under Hull, he was, among other things, in charge of coordinating economic matters in the Department of State. Many people in the Department had the impression that their duties were identical with his; practically every fourth person considered himself an economic coordinator, or at least an economist. Acheson soon came face-to-face with large, amorphous, intense, prerogative-minded groups, in charge of such matters as trade agreements, the gathering of vital commodities, the collation, analysis, and hashing over of economic data, and the preparation of speeches based upon the collation, analysis, and hashing over of the data that had been collated, analyzed, and hashed over. He also came face to face with stray, isolated groups, some of which had gone without solid food for months. While Acheson was economic coordinator in a State Department of seven thousand employees, and while handling the subsequent hot potatoes, he had an opportunity to learn more about the intricate inner workings of the State Department than any other high Departmental officer within memory. Now that he is Secretary of a State Department with twenty-two thousand employees, this knowledge is of inestimable value. "Acheson is one of the few foreign secretaries, in any country, who are not, in a sense, trapped by their departmental experts," a student of foreign policy has observed. During his early years as Assistant Secretary, Acheson many times felt like resigning. He was restrained by his sense of duty and by the notion that he would be doing himself a great disservice if he withdrew a second time from the government.

Except for one trip to Montreal, Acheson remained in this country all during the war. He attended neither of the Roosevelt-Churchill-Stalin conferences, but by the end of the war he had rung up a record for attendance at international conferences in the United States. He had a great deal to do with the formation of the International Bank for Reconstruction and Development (at the Bretton Woods conference), the United Nations Relief and Rehabilitation Administration (at a conference in Atlantic City), and the Food and Agriculture Organization (at a conference in Hot Springs, Arkansas). His most difficult task came each time after the conference was over, when he had to go before congressional committees and plead for the passage of implementing legislation. His approach to a conference was all business. When there is official work to be done, he has a compulsive desire to get it done. To his amusement and occasional dismay, he discovered that a great many international conferences had a way of turning into *Kaffeeklatsche,* at which old League of Nations hands would renew acquaintance and talk over the bittersweet days on the shores of Lake Geneva. He displayed a cultivated impatience less toward the time-consuming social side of the conferences than toward their tendency to postpone action by wandering down procedural bypaths. Perhaps in part because of this attitude, some of Acheson's critics accuse him of being unsympathetic toward the United Nations. Many other observers see no possible basis for this accusation. In the spring of 1949, he informally told the members of the United States delegation to the General Assembly that he was heartily in favor of the foreign ministers' attending the opening session as "an outward and visible sign of our inward and spiritual grace."

Acheson occasionally became conference-happy, notably at the gathering that resulted in the formulation of UNRRA. At Atlantic City, he worked eighteen hours a day, rising at seven-fifteen, having breakfast with assistants to plan the day's program, meeting all day in conference sessions, having a cocktail around five or six with delegates, eating dinner with his assistants, and then returning to his hotel room for four or five more hours of studying tables, charts, and reports. One night, reading a speech over the radio, he deviated from his prepared text and announced that UNRRA aid of two billion dollars was contemplated. The text said two billion five hundred million. A newspaperman later asked him what had become of the missing half billion. "A split-second decision after a martini," Acheson said. Although noticeably weary by that time, he insisted upon exactitude in the wording of UNRRA agreements, suggesting, for example, that a phrase in a paragraph that dealt with eligible beneficiaries be changed from "expectant mothers" to "pregnant women." "A maiden aunt of fifty-one told me once that she was an expectant mother," he told a group of foreign delegates. "What you mean here is 'pregnant women.'" The delegates, aware that they were dealing with a man with a Continental mind, willingly made the change.

Patience, a prime requisite for a successful career in diplomacy, came slowly to Acheson, by nature an impatient man. His wartime dealings with Russian representatives taught him the necessity for patience. "In the old days before the war, Dean would argue quite eloquently with many of his young associates," one of his friends has said. "The Soviet system was a tyranny, he would say, and make no mistake about it. But once the coalition had been struck—and he believed it was the only course to victory—he determined to do everything he could to see it through. The Russians would haggle over some point, get it settled—or appear to get it settled—and then be back in his office two or three days later for more haggling. Dean gritted his teeth, kept his temper, explained and explained and explained that we were friends, that we wanted to be friends, then and after the war." Patience became a pressing personal necessity in Acheson's life in 1944, when his daughter Mary was stricken with a lung ailment and went to Saranac to recuperate. Mary, who had been doing code-breaking in the War Department, had been in the habit of spending a half hour over a bedtime glass of milk with her father in the kitchen. She would tell her father what was on her mind, and he would tell her some of the things that were on his. These sessions had become a ritual, and when Mary went to Saranac, a large gap was left in both their lives. Acheson knew that only a slow cure would restore his daughter's health. What his temperament demanded was a quick one. He resolved that he would never betray his impatience or his anxiety. Every evening while Mary was in Saranac—she was there for more than a year—he sat down at the hour he used to talk with her in the kitchen and wrote her a long, chatty letter. To cheer her, he began each letter with a family joke. Acheson took up gardening to occupy his mind. He began to raise dahlias and gladioli and became expert in the growing of bulbs. "Mary's illness marked a tremendous crisis in Dean's life," an old friend said recently. "It was perhaps more important to him as a statesman than meeting with hundreds of diplomats or tackling hundreds of ticklish world problems. He became reconciled to slow, hard answers to difficult questions."

As Assistant Secretary of State, Acheson's salary was nine thousand dollars a year, a small figure compared with his income at the bar. In the summer of 1945, he told Secretary Byrnes that he could no longer afford to continue in office. Both Byrnes and President Truman urged him to remain, but he said that his decision was final. He went to Saranac to visit his daughter. Byrnes telephoned him there and said that President Truman refused to accept his resignation, insisted that he accept the post of Under-Secretary, and had already dispatched his private plane to bring him back to Washington. Although the new job paid only a thousand dollars more a year than the old one, Acheson found it impossible to resist; it would place him near the highest level of government service. He accepted the appointment and flew back.

Byrnes was out of the country two hundred and forty-five of the five hundred and sixty-two days he held office leaving Acheson behind as Acting Secretary. One of the most important questions he faced was the problem of international control of atomic energy. He knew that the creation of the atomic bomb upset the whole relationship of nation to nation. World peace, he felt, depended to a large extent upon a swift, intelligent attack on the problem. If an atomic-arms race could be avoided by the setting up of an international agency devoted to the gradual, safeguarded sharing of atomic knowledge by peacefully inclined nations, the world, he was sure, had a reasonable chance of preserving itself. Byrnes appointed Acheson chairman of the Secretary of State's Committee on Atomic Energy, which included Vannevar Bush, James B. Conant, Major General Leslie R. Groves, and John J. McCloy. This committee appointed a Board of Consultants, consisting of David E. Lilienthal, as chairman, Chester I. Barnard, Dr. J. Robert Oppenheimer, Dr. Charles A. Thomas, and Harry A. Winne, to prepare a report "anticipating favorable action by the United Nations Organization on the proposal for the establishment of a commission to consider the problems arising as to the control of atomic energy" and "to study the subject of controls and safeguards necessary to protect this government."

While the Board of Consultants was preparing its report, Acheson learned as much as he could about atoms. He asked Dr. Oppenheimer to stop by his house from time to time in the evening and give him an informal lecture on the subject. Oppenheimer would turn up with blackboard and chalk. Each of the sessions lasted for several hours. Oppenheimer has since remarked that Acheson grasped the essentials with astonishing speed. When the Board of Consultants brought in its report, Acheson ironed out some major differences of opinion between his committee and the Board of Consultants. Several members of the Secretary of State's Committee felt that the report was excellent as far as it went but that it should give a more detailed exposition of methods of setting up and operating international control. "You have a fine ship here," Dr. Conant is said to have remarked, "but how are you going to get it in the water?" Overcoming some opposition, Acheson convinced everybody that a chapter, to be composed by Dr. Oppenheimer, should be added to the report to cover this ground. "Acheson was a remarkable chairman, especially in the way he helped us reach workable compromises," a member of the Board of Consultants said not long ago. "He helped, too, by stressing in his introduction to the report that it was not a final paper but, as he put it, 'a place to begin, a foundation on which to build.'" The report, known as the Acheson-Lilienthal Report, was the basis of the proposals made by the United States to the United Nations in the Baruch Plan, accepted by the UN Atomic Energy Commission, and approved by the General Assembly, for control of atomic energy. The Russian government, however, has not approved, and for the moment, at least, the atomic situation is deadlocked.

When Marshall succeeded Byrnes as Secretary of State, in 1947, Acheson agreed to remain in the State Department for only six more months. This time, he said, he would not change his mind; his financial situation demanded a return to the law. Like Byrnes, Marshall was away from the State Department much of the time, and again Acheson was Acting Secretary. Marshall, Acheson, and Will Clayton, who was roving about Europe for the Department on economic missions, all independently reached the conclusion that Europe's economy could be restored only by large-scale aid from the United States. Marshall realized this from the moment he began to deal with the Russians; their policy, he felt, was to stall European recovery. Clayton, traveling from country to country, came to understand Europe's need for dollars to strengthen shattered currencies and replace destroyed factories. Acheson, at home, scanning reports and surveying the problem from the vantage point of distance, is credited in Washington with having evolved many of the details of the Marshall Plan. The first inkling that it had been formulated was contained in a speech Acheson made before the Delta Council, a gathering of farmers and planters, at Cleveland, Mississippi, in May 1947. President Truman was to have addressed the group, but he was unable to attend, and asked Acheson to speak in his place. Instead of preparing a routine speech, Acheson, at Marshall's suggestion, jotted down some of Marshall's, Truman's, and his own thoughts on United States aid to Europe. Armed with a rough draft of a speech, he climbed into the President's plane and flew to Mississippi, putting the finishing touches on his speech while aloft. The plane landed in a large field outside Cleveland, where a welcoming committee greeted Acheson and took him to the schoolhouse for a fried-chicken lunch and then to the school gymnasium, where several hundred farmers, in galluses, were awaiting his talk. Acheson removed his coat, discarded his prepared text, and spoke to the group earnestly and at length. The gist of his remarks added up to the Marshall Plan. Acheson went back to the field in a station wagon and, while the plane was being warmed up, drank a mint julep prepared by his hosts. A month later, Marshall, feeling that the time was ripe for a pronouncement by the Secretary of State himself, delivered an address at the Harvard Commencement exercises, dropping a large hint that if European nations were interested, the United States was willing to give them aid.

Acheson resigned from the State Department in July of 1947 and returned to his law firm. He especially regretted severing relations with Marshall, with whom he had worked in a harmonious atmosphere occasionally lacking during the regimes of other Secretaries of State. For the next year and a half, although pleased to be with his old partners again, he had a gnawing desire to get back into public life. "Once a man has tasted public power, he probably never forgets the taste," a former law associate of Acheson's said recently. Acheson pleaded several civil-rights cases and, as vice-chairman, under Herbert Hoover, devoted a great deal of time to the work of the Commission on Organization of the Executive Branch of the Government, paying special attention to increasing the efficiency of the State Department. When Truman was elected, in November 1948, he almost immediately asked Acheson if he would become his Secretary of State in January. Acheson, surprised, but knowing that Marshall intended to resign, accepted with solemn enthusiasm. "It has taken years and years," he told a close friend, "but now I am on my own."

The after-dark activities of Rudolph, who has been for over twenty-five years the official chauffeur of the Secretary of State, indicate the extent of a Secretary of State's social life. Under Hull, Rudolph was certain of going home every evening, and staying home, once he had driven the Secretary to the Wardman Park Hotel, where he lived in Washington. When Stettinius succeeded Hull, Rudolph remarked to a State Department colleague, "The honeymoon's over." Stettinius was a gregarious man and spent many evenings visiting friends. Byrnes kept Rudolph on call nearly every evening. Since becoming Secretary, Acheson has spent an average of only one night a week visiting friends or attending social functions. Unless there is a conclave of high-ranking foreign diplomats, and the concomitant schedule of full-dress events, Acheson usually stays home at night. These days, high government officials rarely give formal dinners at home; that custom died with the war. If Acheson is obliged to entertain visiting dignitaries formally, he does so at a hotel. He has had his name removed from the telephone directory, and only the most important phone calls are relayed home to him by the Department of State. Most evenings, he and Mrs. Acheson have a quiet supper together and talk a while. One or more of the Acheson children may drop by, and then the Secretary will talk with them or maybe read aloud to them for a half hour. Felix Frankfurter may telephone to read Acheson a passage of a book he is reading. Acheson, in turn, may read Frankfurter a passage from a book *he* is reading. Occasionally, a friend stops in for a chat. Sometime before ten o'clock, Acheson usually goes into his study to put in several more hours of work. The Achesons spend almost every weekend at their house in the country. "I try to see that the Secretary has a proper weekend—without interruptions," Mrs. Acheson says. They drive there on Saturday afternoon and remain until Sunday night, the Secretary pottering about the farm in slacks and sport shirt. Lately, he has become interested in old furniture and has installed a small carpenter shop, where he hopes eventually to turn out replicas of antique chairs and tables. During the last few months, he has found himself taking so much State Department work along with him that his achievements up to now have not gone beyond a few wall brackets and other small knickknacks.

When friends make an early after-dinner call on Acheson in Georgetown, they usually find him sitting erect in a large upholstered easy chair by the fireplace in the living room. The room is an elegantly, comfortable picture-book room, with large windows overlooking a brick-walled garden, soft draperies and lights, oil paintings, vases filled with flowers, and an English-country-house dignity. Acheson rarely discusses the broader aspects of his job with his friends. He is more inclined to relate a humorous incident of the day or to discuss the work of his visitors. Once in a while, though, he will speak for a moment or two about some of the problems that concern him most deeply. This happened one evening recently, when he and a friend were having a quiet talk about family life. "When you come right down to it, the purpose of foreign policy is to preserve the freedom of our homes," he said, "and also the freedom to do one's work, or move on and do one's work somewhere else. There are millions throughout the world with the same aspirations—to be allowed to live out their lives in their own way." The Secretary of State thoughtfully pulled at his mustache. The Secretary and his mustache looked equally calm and resolute. "War would end all this," he said. "War would mean regimentation—every man assigned to a hard task, dispersed industries, human beings living underground in caves like beasts, a nightmare. It would mean the very end of all freedom. Peace is freedom, and freedom is our life."

November 1949

CHAPTER 9

PLEASE CLEAR
THE AISLES

I AM NOT A BETTING MAN, but I am willing to wager a new Philco refrigerator, complete with cheese keeper, against a Westinghouse ice tray that the 1952 Republican National Convention will henceforth be known as the Television Convention. Throughout the proceedings, television was unquestionably the leading candidate. All sides wooed it, sought it out, bargained for its favors, and generally pampered it. Early in the convention, it became apparent that both the Taft and the Eisenhower forces recognized that the most important delegates in Chicago were the dozens of cameras perched all over the city—overlooking the teeming convention floor itself, in the great hotels where the candidates had their headquarters, on the streets outside the amphitheatre, and in the studios specially built for the occasion—always relentlessly prying and probing every which way. As I sat in front of my screen at home, it seemed to me that I could detect a difference in the television strategy of the two camps. The Taft plan, I got the feeling, was bold and simple: to present venerable symbols of the republic, who would evoke in the eye and mind of the viewer a sense of identification with the past, on the assumption—a not unreasonable one—that the average citizen and the average delegate yearn for the past and think of it lovingly as an untroubled refuge from the tumultuous present. The Eisenhower people, I thought, had a different notion of the way to approach television. They were, for the most part, new faces, and they spoke less of the past than of the present and the future. Almost to a man, they abandoned circumlocution, and although their speeches dripped with indignation, they dealt surprisingly often, considering that this was a political convention, with facts instead of fancies.

The cameras, observing this battle, maintained a wonderful impartiality. All week long, they stared away, like large, unblinking, unthinking eyes. If a man had something to say, he got up and said it, and the cameras recorded his picture and the microphones picked up his words. There were moments—especially during the tense voting sessions on the seating of the disputed delegates—when I found it hard to believe that human beings were controlling the cameras, so direct and unbiased a view did they present. The temptation on the part of the cameramen to indulge their own feelings by slipping in a tricky partisan shot must have been compelling, but I cannot recall any such thing happening. As a result, the viewer felt himself a part of the convention, and this viewer even beguiled himself, on occasion, into thinking that he was entitled to cast a vote when the roll was called.

The direction and camerawork in Chicago were nothing short of magnificent and had about them an almost incredible personal quality and sense of intimacy. One felt as though one were standing beside a speaker on the podium, as though one were seated among a delegation on the floor, as though, in the course of demonstrations in favor of particular candidates, one were actually down there marching through the crowded aisles. One got to know certain strangers rather well, as though one were confined with them aboard ship during a crossing of the Atlantic. I think, for instance, that I know a great deal about Walter Hallanan, the strapping and imposing West Virginian who served as temporary chairman of the convention. For hours at a stretch, Mr. Hallanan made no move, no flicker of the eyebrow or turn of the head, that I was not privy to; as time went along, I grew to have a high regard for his masterly parliamentary hand and what seemed to me to be his utter impartiality in the matter of rulings from the chair. I also had the feeling—shared, I am certain, by thousands of other viewers—that although Mr. Hallanan and I might quarrel violently over some aspects of politics, he would listen and weigh my views and reach a democratic accommodation. As for Governor Dewey, thanks to the camera, which returned to him time and again as though he were a sort of Greek chorus, I think I got to know him much better than, as a resident of his state, I had ever known him before. His role was a most difficult one. He was seated on the floor of the convention, amid the New York delegation, and he was a marked man—a man twice defeated for the Presidency. From time to time, he was the butt of Taft speakers, notably of Senator Dirksen, who attacked him directly for his past failures. Mr. Dewey maintained a good humor, a composure, and an air of dignity that were something more than impressive. And then there were the many other faces—the wiry, thin-faced woman whose enthusiasm for Taft was tempered only by a large pin she wore on her blouse that read, "I Like Everybody"; the old gentleman who slowly waved two handkerchiefs for practically everything and everyone; the Puerto Ricans; the strange bearded man in a leopard-skin suit; the slaphappy girl on the shoulders of her boyfriend; the Warren girls, in their box, looking quite as pretty as they are supposed to look—and the voices, too, and the accents from every part of the nation, reminding us of ourselves.

I suppose the greatest contribution made by the television coverage—and this is a point that will undoubtedly be discussed by students of government for years—was the realization it gave all viewers of the complexity of selecting a Presidential candidate. Certainly the so-called smoke-filled room tends to lose its air of mystery and secrecy when one is, so to speak, sitting, if not in the room itself, at least in the room down the corridor. The problem suddenly becomes less one of intrigue than one of argument and parliamentary procedure. The contending forces, apparently so irreconcilable, are clearly circumscribed by the rules that govern their conduct. Patience is required, not only of the television viewer, the citizen at home, but of the delegates assembled, and the democratic process becomes not only a spectacle but part of ourselves.

July 1952

CHAPTER 10

BACK TO CHICAGO

Television altered the entire pattern of American politics. Nobody could possibly grasp the revolutionary impact of *seeing* everything. Before television, events always took place in the smoke-filled back room, but now the pols realized that the back room could be brought into the nation's living room. So they kept what went on in the back room out of sight, and developed masterly techniques of visual deceit. It was not long before the spinmeisters realized that a stubble of beard or a genuine teardrop could destroy a candidate for life. Be an actor, or drop dead. (We actually elected an actor—twice). The 1952 Democratic Convention was just about the last of the reasonably unadorned gatherings; it's a period piece, with an innocence you won't find later. In fairness, I must say that I see (early 2000) a glimmer of light. By popular demand, some attempt at real debating is taking place, but don't bet the barn on it.

I AM A REASONABLY OLD EYE at this television game by now, I guess, but the coverage of the Democratic National Convention last week beat anything I had ever seen on land, at sea, or in the air. The tiny screen at our house was alight for days and nights on end, meals were eaten in front of the set, friends came and went—some for Stevenson, some for Harriman, and some for Barkley, including a voluble Southern lady who burst into tears during the Vice-President's speech and sang "My Old Kentucky Home" until silenced by the local chair. The only dissenter throughout the proceedings was a five-year-old boy who boards at our place and who, frustrated almost beyond endurance by his continuing inability to make contact with Howdy Doody, kept demanding, "When is this stinky program going to end?" Now that it *has* ended, I find myself wondering just what there was about it that kept me so entranced. Unquestionably, one factor—and this, of course, was true of the Republican proceedings as well—was the mechanical miracle of the thing. I felt this most strongly on Friday afternoon, during the early balloting. The Missouri delegation was being polled individually on the floor, and the cameras were focused on the delegates. I happened to be watching an NBC station when, without warning, the convention floor disappeared and I saw a long black limousine slide up beside a huge airplane. An announcer broke in to say that the President of the United States was at that moment about to fly from Washington to Chicago and that we were to witness his departure. Seconds later, I heard again the voices of the Missouri delegation answering the roll call and hollering the names of this candidate and that, but on the screen the President was stepping out of his car, waving genially to the crowd at the Washington airport, and mounting the ramp to his plane. As he turned for a last salute, I heard from Chicago the voice of his alternate, Mr. Gavin, announcing that his—and the President's—choice was Governor Stevenson, of Illinois. It was uncanny and it was wonderful.

Still, there was more to it than the mechanics of television, and as I think back on the whole business, I'm sure that—as in the case of the Republican meeting—the important thing was one's sense of participation in matters that concern one deeply. Television, covering affairs of this sort, makes the viewer a member of a community vastly larger than his own without demanding that he sacrifice any of his individuality. It does not require him to judge, nor does it judge him—a nightmare envisioned by George Orwell and mercifully not in prospect. It simply makes it possible for a person, if he so chooses, to be present at, listen to, and watch an event that in the ordinary course of things he would have to depend on others to explain and interpret for him. In a sense, television coverage of a national convention turns the entire nation into a huge town meeting, which one can attend, ponder over, and depart from with one's opinions still one's own.

The Democrats in charge of the proceedings at Chicago made it known, both in the press and over the air, that they had observed the Republican Convention on television and that they wished to avoid some of the errors they felt the Republicans had made on it. For one thing, they said the Republicans had been wrong in not permitting a camera to face the speakers on the platform head on, which meant that there could be only profile shots of them. So a huge platform was erected directly in front of the speakers' rostrum, enabling us to see the orators full face. I don't think it made one bit of difference. The Democratic high command also announced that it was going to avoid the distracting effect—or what it considered the distracting effect during the Republican do—of people moving about behind and to the sides of the speakers, and consequently it went to great lengths to keep the floaters out of range of the cameras. I don't think that this made one bit of difference, either. Once the convention got under way, the people on the floor and on the platform became so interested in what they were doing or saying—so passionate and involved and alive— that the viewer at home ignored everything else on the screen. This was especially true when Governor Stevenson made his acceptance speech early Saturday morning. I even felt that the often stupefying pollings of individual delegates, which many people seem to have resented on the grounds that they held up the proceedings but which were, in truth, the proceedings themselves, were irresistible, being a manifestation of the right of every delegate—and, by extension, every citizen—to take a direct part in the choosing of his President.

Well, things have quieted down around our place; the little boarder, twice displaced during the past month, has reestablished his beach-head in front of the tiny screen and has renewed his friendship with Howdy Doody and all the other causes he feels so deeply about. I don't think I'll try to explain to him just yet that his loss has been the country's gain.

August 1952

CHAPTER 11

LONG WAIT

OUR MAN STANLEY DROPPED BY, somewhat haughtily, on his way from the first Eisenhower Inaugural Ball in Washington to the shooting box of a friend near Lynn, Massachusetts, and left the following communication:

Tell Buckley at Guaranty Trust to do nothing about Union Carbide until he hears from me. Decided early on Inauguration Day to attend ball at Georgetown University gymnasium rather than one at armory. Gymnasium in posh part of town, armory on other side of tracks. Always prefer posh. Why not? Wore more stuff than Franz Josef. Had biggest blue-and-white badge ever manufactured, reading, "Working Press"; had white tag reading, "Inaugural Ball Messenger"; had green-and-white tag reading, "Bearer May Cross Pennsylvania Avenue" (didn't *want* to cross Pennsylvania Avenue); had green card reading, "Courier." Also had lozenge-shaped red-and-white card saying, "Police Will Pass This Vehicle." Had no vehicle. At 10 P.M., telephoned old-line diplomat friend who had vehicle but no lozenge-shaped card.

Drove to gymnasium with him, he resplendent in white tie and tails, I semiresplendent in black tie, blue coat, dinner jacket, and homburg. Old-line diplomat wore no hat or coat; said he was certain hatcheck arrangements would be fouled up and no one would get hat or coat back for at least four years. Sailed up to floodlit redbrick gym and walked under wedding-type canopy to front door. Diplomat speedily admitted. I was told to use side door. Blessing in disguise, since door led to empty room with grand piano. Placed coat and homburg inside grand piano, closed top, and went down to gym floor. Hell of a place to play basketball. Guy Lombardo and orchestra signing off on huge stage at one end of gym. Place beautifully decorated in blue and gold, colors of Presidential flag. Place three-quarters filled with distinguished ladies and gentlemen. More hoop skirts than in *Gone With the Wind*. Many gentlemen with medals hanging around their necks. Felt like a fool without one. Haven't won a medal since high school. Many floor boxes, looking like cattle stalls at county fair. These almost filled. Spotted Herbert Hoover in upper-tier box overlooking gym floor. Hoover pink and white. He waved to crowd. Crowd waved back. Crowd sentimental about Hoover. Long time no see at Inaugural Ball.

Couples now dancing on floor to music of Noble Sissle. Sissle introduced W. C. Handy, who played "St. Louis Blues" on trumpet. Man with red riband around waist and six hundred medals pinned to jacket asked me who Handy was. Told him. *"Mon Dieu!"* he said. Handy finished playing and left stage. Adolphe Menjou took center of stage. Suave. He said long, arid twenty-year period was over now. He said end was worth waiting for. He said he intended to have fine time, and urged everybody there to have fine time, too. Place crowding up, fewer and fewer people able to dance. Refreshments pretty meagre. No hooch; just two small fountains at stage end of gym spouting orange punch. Drank two tiny paper cups filled with stuff. Fifty cents. Serious inflationary problem, but this no night to quibble.

Around midnight, isolated groups dancing on fringes of floor. Mass of people stopped dead in their tracks. Barely any movement in entire gymnasium. Jack Morton and orchestra now on stage, playing to immobile throng. Vice-President Nixon and wife suddenly entered

Presidential box. Nixon sat down, stood up, sat down, stood up again. Crowd showed restrained enthusiasm. Nixon needed shave. Mrs. Nixon looked pale and pretty. Young lady with two paper cups of orange punch pushed way slowly through crowd, spilled them down neck of elderly gentleman wearing three-foot badge reading, "Inaugural Committee." "Terribly, terribly sorry," said young lady. Elderly gentleman turned to elderly gentleman beside him. "George," he said, "I've been waiting twenty years for this, and I don't think I'm going to live through the night." Voice from loudspeaker urged people not to smoke on floor. Marine colonel standing beside me apologized for sticking his finger in my eye. Young lady in hoop skirt told me she thought she was going to faint. Crush from rear pushed two elderly gentlemen, Marine colonel, lady in hoop skirt, and me almost directly under Presidential box. Mr. and Mrs. Dulles entered box adjoining the Nixons. Dulles bowed, waved his hands like a world statesman. Crowd perked up. Two elderly gentlemen began to talk politics. One smiled at me and said he was glad so many young people had turned up for Ball. He said Republicans had great opportunities and responsibilities. "Among other things," he said, "we must look out for the needy, especially in medical care and that sort of thing." Told him this sounded like Socialism to me. Lady in hoop skirt said forty women had fainted on floor. Saltonstall pushed way past McCarthy, sweating profusely in a box. Thomas J. Watson pushed way past Saltonstall. Thought I saw the elder Morgan.

About twelve-thirty, President and Mrs. Eisenhower arrived. Tremendous cheer from floor. Air Force Band played "Hail to the Chief." Ike solemn until music over, then broke into grin. He looked fine, just fine. Sat down, drummed fingers on rail of box; preoccupied and thoughtful man. Mamie full of fun, spotted friends on floor, waved frantically, tugged at Ike's sleeve. He tried to recognize them but couldn't. Son John put on dark-rimmed glasses, peered at crowd. Spit and image of the President. Whole family elegant-looking, relaxed. Crush on floor impossible. Seven thousand people just standing around staring up at Presidential box. Lauritz Melchior stepped onto the stage and sang "The Star-Spangled Banner." Gladys Swarthout stepped onto the stage and sang "Bless This House." Charles Wilson stepped into Ike's box. Little confab together. Moment of decision? West Point Cadet Glee Club stepped onto the stage and sang song to Mamie and Ike. Marine colonel stepped on feet of lady in hoop skirt, and lady in hoop skirt stepped on me. About one-fifteen, Ike and Mamie left for new house on Pennsylvania Avenue. Certainly hope they will be happy there.

January 1953

CHAPTER 12

MAN FROM WISCONSIN

AFTER HIS INTERROGATION by Senator Joseph R. McCarthy a few weeks ago, General Ralph Zwicker, the commandant of Camp Kilmer, turned to his aides, according to the papers, and remarked, "Boys, now you've had an education." I felt the same way the other night after watching Edward R. Murrow's half-hour report on the Senator, over his weekly "See It Now" program, sponsored by the Aluminum Company of America (CBS, 10:30–11 P.M. on Tuesdays). Mr. Murrow brought off an extraordinary feat of journalism by the simple expedient of compiling a pictorial history of the Senator, complete with sound track, that showed him as he has performed in a variety of places and under a variety of circumstances during the past few years. Mr. Murrow let the Senator do most, but not all, of the work. We saw McCarthy speaking in Milwaukee, we saw him speaking in Philadelphia, we watched him conduct an investigation of the Voice of America, we heard a tape recording of a speech he delivered in Charleston, West Virginia, and we watched some of his operations during the 1952 Presidential campaign. We also got a pretty good look at the fellow—the best that I, for one, have ever got. To begin with, he's a big man, with big hands and a large head. Most of the time, he has a petulant, droop-jaw expression, as though, at the very instant he was all set to challenge everybody in the place to step outside, he was convinced that everybody in the place was about to jump him. He has a soft, almost silky, droning voice, which he tries somewhat too obviously to control. His laugh is frightening. He uses his hands a great deal for emphasis. While interrogating a witness, he gives the impression that all light, all truth, and all honesty belong at the moment to him alone, but then destroys the impression by appearing, curiously and unexpectedly, to be uncertain of his next move.

Mr. Murrow's intent was to pick the Senator up in a series of contradictions. He quoted the Senator as having declared in Milwaukee seventeen months ago, "If this fight against Communism is made a fight between America's two great political parties, the American people know that one of those parties will be destroyed, and the Republic cannot endure very long as a one-party system." He then let us hear the remarks of the Senator in Charleston on February 4th of this year: "The issue between the Republicans and Democrats is clearly drawn. It has been deliberately drawn by those who have been in charge of twenty years of treason. The hard fact is that those who wear the label 'Democrat' wear it with the stain of a historic betrayal." We saw the Senator in many moods—arrogant, aroused, fierce, and humble. To depict this last mood, Murrow threw a shot on the screen of a political dinner somewhere. An elderly gentleman at the speaker's table who was introducing the Senator became almost overwhelmed with emotion. He said he could not express what was in his heart, and he reached across the table and plucked some flowers from a floral arrangement, remarking:

> Ah, 'tis but a dainty flower I bring you,
> Yes, 'tis but a violet, glistening with dew,
> But still in its heart there lie beauties concealed.
> So in our heart our love for you lies unrevealed.

McCarthy arose, gulping, and said, "You know, I used to pride myself on the idea that I was a bit tough, especially over the past eighteen or nineteen months, when we have been kicked around and bull-whipped and damned. I didn't think that I could be touched very deeply. But tonight, frankly, my cup and my heart are so full I can't talk to you." And he turned away, almost in tears.

Throughout the program, Mr. Murrow quietly added comments of his own. He made no attempt to hide his strong feelings of distaste and shock at the methods and language of the Senator. Murrow is, of course, a master of pictorial presentation and rarely forgets that television is designed for the eye as well as the ear. His most effective use of pictorial technique, it seemed to me, came in his discussion of the Senator's charge that "extreme Left Wing elements of press and radio" were attacking his committee over the Zwicker affair. Mr. Murrow had before him two stacks of newspapers, and, pointing to one, he said, "Of the fifty large-circulation newspapers in the country, these are the Left Wing papers that criticized." Then, pointing to the other, he said, "These are the ones that supported him. The ratio is about three to one against the Senator. Now let us look at some of these Left Wing papers that criticized the Senator." Thereupon he read editorial excerpts from the Chicago *Tribune,* the New York *Times,* the Washington *Times-Herald,* the New York *Herald Tribune,* the Washington *Star,* the Milwaukee *Journal,* the *World-Telegram & Sun,* and others.

Just before the conclusion of his program, Mr. Murrow fixed the audience with an almost glassy stare and read, solemnly and deliberately, an editorial he had composed for the occasion. I thought that he was especially impressive when he remarked, "This is no time for men who oppose Senator McCarthy's methods to keep silent, or for those who approve. We can deny our heritage and our history, but we cannot escape responsibility for the result. There is no way for a citizen of a republic to abdicate his responsibilities. . . . The actions of the Junior Senator from Wisconsin have caused alarm and dismay amongst our allies abroad and given considerable comfort to our enemies, and whose fault is that? Not really his; he didn't create this situation of fear, he merely exploited it, and rather successfully. Cassius was right: 'The fault, dear Brutus, is not in our stars, but in ourselves. . . .' Good night, and good luck."

March 1954

CHAPTER 13

BRAIN

WITH A MECHANICAL, NONPARTISAN SMILE, Mr. Stanley stepped into the office the day after the 1956 election:

Spent Election Night in company of Univac, giant Remington-Rand electronic brain, at Remington-Rand Building, on lower Fourth Avenue. Univac that people saw on CBS television not actual Univac —just blinking, flashing facsimile of control board of brain itself. Real brain sweating like Einstein downtown, giving results that were subsequently phoned to CBS correspondents at studio uptown, then read over air. Went downtown after supper, entered control room for big brain through closely guarded door. Room a madhouse. Close to a hundred human brains, attached to bodies, occupied room, some bending over teletype machines, others poring over stacks of papers at desks, others standing before restaurant-refrigerator-type machines with glass fronts and whirring discs inside. Control boards every-where—red, green, amber. Terrifying. Was mercifully taken in hand by Dr. Max Woodbury, of New York University's College of Engineering Mathematics Department. Dr. Woodbury, a tall, tense brain, with minute reddish-brown mustache—one of several scientists in charge of Univac operation. "Univac has a great mind," he said. His voice was filled with awe. "All these people are servicing Univac, helping her to reach her conclusions," he said. "We began stuffing statistics into Univac in 1952 and 1954. Originally, we went back to Bryan and free silver for statistics, but they didn't seem to have any appreciable pertinence, so we confined ourselves ultimately to data from 1928 onward. Mostly Presidential-election figures—data from states and districts, paying special attention to unique counties, such as Wayne County, Michigan; Polk County, Iowa; San Francisco County; and the five boroughs of New York. Univac knows a unique county when she sees one," he said cryptically.

"Brain working now?" I asked.

"Working?" he said. "Like a dream."

"How does she work?" I asked.

"Briefly," said Dr. Woodbury, "raw material comes in from the teletypes, is processed by people at that circular desk, is broken down into precincts—possibility of human error here, you know—and is transferred to Univac digital recording magnetic tape. The tapes are placed in one of the ten servos, and then translated to Univac herself. Univac compares current data with accumulated data and comes out with the answers." Courier bearing white slip of paper interrupted Dr. Woodbury. Dr. Woodbury scanned paper. "Univac predicts, on basis of one million votes counted, three hundred and ninety-eight electoral votes for Ike, sixty-eight for Stevenson, with the balance in doubt. Perfectly splendid! Right on the beam! Univac is willing to go a hundred to one for Eisenhower! And now I'll show you Univac herself—the works—through glass, of course."

Went to end of room and looked through window at what seemed like dozen or more airplane engines, millions of coils and lights. "The brain!" said Dr. Woodbury. "We have to cool her off with air." Quiet-looking man stepped up. "Meet Dr. John Mauchly," said Dr. Woodbury. "Dr. Mauchly, here, is a co-inventor of Univac."

"Univac costs one million dollars to purchase outright," said Dr. Mauchly. "Twenty-five thousand dollars a month to rent." Told Dr. Mauchly I'd think it over. "Univac is going smoothly," said Dr. Mauchly.

"One thing worries me," said Dr. Woodbury. "Univac says Tennessee is going Democratic, I say Tennessee is going Republican." Courier arrived with United Press dispatch that Tennessee was going Republican. "The machine is slightly wrong," said Dr. Woodbury, tugging at his mustache.

Evening wore on, machines whirred, lights flashed. On basis of 2,600,000 votes counted, Univac predicted 383 electoral votes for Eisenhower, 90 for Stevenson, 58 doubtful. On basis of 3,773,000 votes counted, Univac predicted 405 electoral votes for Eisenhower, 81 for Stevenson, 45 in doubt. Drs. Mauchly and Woodbury beamed. Courier arrived and whispered something into Dr. Woodbury's ear. "The machine has goofed," said Dr. Woodbury. "Mechanical failure, but just possibly an input goof."

"She has become persnickety about accepting some data," said Dr. Mauchly. "Often, she regurgitates unacceptable data into her post-mortem file."

"That's how we catch the goofs," said Dr. Woodbury. He was now tugging fiercely at his mustache.

"The brain is smart," said Dr. Mauchly, his voice like cold steel, "but the brain is also stupid. Stuff her with something wrong and she'll go right ahead with it."

"Sometimes a surprising trend disturbs her, and then she has to make a decision," says Dr. Woodbury. "Often, she says, 'I will not accept this decision,' and that's where the post-mortem file comes in."

"Really, *we* make the value judgments," said Dr. Mauchly.

"No," said Dr. Woodbury, "we do the creation."

"I can give her the rules," said Dr. Mauchly.

"I feel we are following the decision rules," said Dr. Woodbury. Group of anxious technicians huddled over a control board. Red lights were flashing wildly. "Error lights," said Dr. Woodbury.

"Easy to blame the machinery," said Dr. Mauchly. "Could be human failure."

"The trouble is in the Senate," said Dr. Woodbury. "She's goofed on the Senate."

Drs. Woodbury and Mauchly joined technicians at control board. I went home and listened to returns on radio. Eisenhower by landslide.

November 1956

CHAPTER 14

from THE MAYOR

"Don't Honk, Bobby—the Man Is a Voter"

When I wrote the Profile of Mayor Robert Wagner, we were across-the-street neighbors, and had many friends in common. I often visited Gracie Mansion. The last time I saw him, lunching at a midtown club shortly before he died in 1991, he asked me a typical Wagner question. "Everything under control?" he said.

SEVERAL ANALYSTS OF AMERICAN political life have reached the conclusion that the office of Mayor of the City of New York is second in importance only to that of the President of the United States. Many students of the subject feel that physically it is an even more gruelling one. In an indefinable but unmistakable way, the forbidding austerity of what has been called the greatest elective office in the history of the world protects the President from the swirling rough-and-tumble in which his subordinates and would-be subordinates are perpetually embroiled. And in case anyone should fail to be impressed by that austerity, there is always the Secret Service. Held in check by one or the other of these restraints, people simply do not run up and tap the President on the shoulder and ask for an appointment the next day.

No such protection is afforded the Mayor of the City of New York. Big though the city has become, its citizens still have a kind of neighborly feeling toward whoever is occupying the mayor's office, and no matter how diligently his staff tries to guard against a break in his schedule, informal intrusions and interruptions occur all the time. As the counterpart of the President's Secret Service, the mayor, of course, has his bodyguards, but Wagner, having been brought up in the school of municipal politics and thus been made aware that everybody— absolutely everybody—is a voter, would not think of holding himself physically aloof from the clamoring throng. Besides, the Mayor is not the kind of man who spends long, solitary hours poring over official papers or formulating and reformulating theories of municipal government; essentially gregarious to start with, he needs contact with the people of the city to guide him, and the result is that anyone who manages to get close enough to make his voice heard is likely to be told, "O.K. Drop in tomorrow." A person who has thus received the nod turns up the next day at City Hall, repeats the spoken invitation to whoever will listen, persists through a phalanx of secretaries and assistants, and, more often than not, succeeds in gumming up the Mayor's schedule. The court of final appeal for these suppliants, as they beg for a minute, just a minute, of the Mayor's time, is Wagner's private secretary, Miss Anne Kelly. "Added starters—that's what I call them," she says of the people who manage to persuade her that they have a bona-fide invitation from the Mayor. Miss Kelly, who was Wagner's secretary when he was Borough President of Manhattan and whose political instincts are almost as sensitive as his, knows it is an ironclad rule that if the Mayor actually has told a man to stop by, the man must be seen by the Mayor, no matter what. From her point of view, added starters wouldn't be so bad if the Mayor would only limit his interviews with them to the minute they ask for. But Wagner is not made that way, and once he gets to talking with a man, the minutes begin to pile up.

The Mayor contrives to have dinner at home two or three times a week, but this does not necessarily mean that he spends these evenings with his family. More likely he will return home for a relatively early dinner and afterward dash off to the first of several public functions he must attend that night, or else, having already made a couple of his scheduled stops, he will drop in at the Mansion for a mid-evening meal and then continue on his way. Wagner and his wife think no more of sitting down to dinner at eleven o'clock than at eight. Whenever they do have dinner together, the Mayor first relaxes with a bourbon or a martini, and then the meal is served by Henry. The Wagners' cook is Mrs. Florence Fahsing, who worked for Senator Wagner for many years and stayed with the family after the Senator's death. Mrs. Fahsing, a jolly Cornish-woman, speaks lovingly of the Mayor's eating habits. In her eyes, every dish she cooks for him is his favorite. "I think his favorite is roast beef and Yorkshire pudding," she said recently. "On the roast beef, he favors horseradish sauce. Steak is his favorite, too. If you want to make him truly happy, you give him one of his favorites—all kinds of homemade soups, such as oxtail or green pea or chicken. I think his real favorite is ham and baked potato. And so is walnut *torte*. My, but he likes walnut *torte!* Or maybe it's ice cream with nuts over it. Yes, that's his special favorite, and he calls it Ice Cream Florence. In honor of me."

The chances are that by the time Wagner reaches the walnut *torte* or the Ice Cream Florence, he is already putting together in his mind the brief message he will deliver half an hour later at a fraternal meeting or a charity ball somewhere in the city. As mayor, Wagner is under immense pressure to make these evening rounds. The banquet invitations he receives average in the vicinity of three hundred a month, and are carefully screened by his executive secretary, Peer. This is an extremely delicate job, since it is obviously impossible for the Mayor to get around the five boroughs fast enough even to look in at all the places he's invited to, and yet, with few exceptions, his would-be hosts are endeavoring to promote worthy causes—civic betterment, philanthropy, religion, patriotism, social service, and so on. In accepting invitations for the Mayor to attend several banquets in one evening,

Peer emphasizes to the various committees in charge that the Mayor will be merely a "dais guest"; that is, he will put in an appearance at the speakers' table, have nothing to eat, say a few words, and thereupon duck out as unobtrusively as possible. The Mayor's evening schedules also include a number of what are known as "drop-ins" at political rallies of one sort or another. A drop-in can, without giving offense, last only six or seven minutes.

Friday nights present the most difficult scheduling problem, since nearly all the district Democratic clubs hold their biggest socials then. Being a politician, the Mayor is at his best at jamborees of this sort, even if he is just doing a drop-in. He has an astonishingly retentive memory—so retentive that some experienced campaigners say they have come across nothing like it since the days when James A. Farley was handshaking his way around the nation in the interests of Franklin D. Roosevelt. "Wagner never forgets a face," one of these old-timers said the other day. "And, of course, he never forgets the name that goes with the face. But that's elementary. It's when he gets into the more intricate details of the life of a guy he hasn't seen in two or three years—and then just for a moment at a crowded rally—that he really begins to shine. He'll meet Joe Doakes at some shindig and remark that he remembers old Joe had a toothache the last time he saw him, back in 1954. Then he'll say, 'Tell me, Joe, how are the two boys, Mac and Bill, and how is the little girl, Joan?' And after Joe beams and tells him, Wagner will say, 'Joan must be about eleven by now, and I recall that Bill had the mumps when I saw you last. Did Mac and Joan get them, too?'" The Mayor's memory keeps a record not only of people's names and faces and the trivia of people's conversations but of the letters people write him. "You know," he will say to Miss Kelly, "about six, seven months ago I had a letter from that fellow who called this morning. It was on white paper, and it had a little yellow thing on top, and blue engraving. It wasn't of any importance, so I suppose we didn't file it, but you might just look and see."

February 1957

CHAPTER 15

LONELY DAY

E LECTION DAY, HERE IN THE CITY, is one of the quietest of all
days. We voted early. We were up and out of the house and headed
for the polls a few minutes before six. Our street was dark and silent,
the air was crisp and brilliant, and the day held promise. We don't
have far to go to reach the polls—a few steps south, past the barber-
shop, the hardware shop, and the tailor shop, and a few steps east,
downhill (with the river at the foot of the hill). On our way south, we
saw the moon, and a faint light in the rear of Mr. Strandbury's store
(he delivers papers); his newsstand was still bare. Turning east, we
saw the river far below, and streaks of blue and orange in the morning
sky. We vote in a luggage shop barely the size of a steamer trunk—a
cramped, cluttered establishment, its floor covered with suitcases,
handbags, and piles of old belts, its walls inexplicably plastered, from
floor to ceiling, with photographs of stars of stage, screen, and television. At one minute to six, we were outside its doors. Two people were
ahead of us—a ruddy-faced man, gray at the temples and wearing a

trim brown topcoat, and a shambling, preoccupied man, coatless. "I vote at the crack of dawn because I like to vote at the crack of dawn," volunteered the ruddy-faced man. "Besides, I work in Brooklyn, and I've got a ride ahead of me." The coatless man had something on his mind. "Somebody has to lose," he said, half to himself. We peered through the window of the store. It was ablaze with light. Precinct workers bustled around a long table, clearing away paper cups and cartons of coffee and opening long, narrow registration books. We spied Jackie Gleason on the wall, smiling, and Bing Crosby beside him. Crosby looked serious. "We Can't Please Everybody But We Try," said a sign in the window. "Deposit Required on All Repair Work." A young policeman was hovering over the voting machine. He unlocked something on one side and tested the green curtain, and the door to the luggage shop was opened. It was precisely six o'clock.

Voting was swift and silent. The ruddy-faced man was a man of decision—in and out and off to Brooklyn. The coatless man took a moment longer, but merely a moment. Then he, too, was off, still preoccupied, still pondering. Our turn came next. For us, voting is a moment of controlled breathlessness. We promise ourself each time to be calm, collected, master of the machine and of ourself, and yet when the curtain closes and we are alone, we pull down the levers with passionate haste. In a moment, we were again outside the booth, having voted. A line had formed behind us, bursting the confines of the luggage shop and spreading out to the street. Nobody said anything.

Day had reached the city with the swiftness of our vote. The sun was over the river's edge now, and the orange-and-blue streaks were becoming a deep and satisfying blue. We walked around for quite a while. It seems to us now that we must have walked around most of the day, as preoccupied as the man who had preceded us into the booth. Fruit stores were the first to open, displaying their seasonal riches—the purple grapes, the shiny red apples. The fruit stands seemed to hold promise. Next, the flower stores opened, and we saw row upon row of mellow, rust-colored pompons. The streets were still silent, and the traffic was light. People were coming out of the apartment houses now, silent and determined, aloof and subdued, acting very much alone even when they were walking with others. We looked in on many school houses, with long lines edging toward the green curtains and the levers and the moment of doing what one thinks is right, and it seemed to us that this was also, perhaps, one of the most private of all days, each man an impressive island unto himself and yet each man a part of the whole. We went down to the office and tried working, but it was no go. The silence of the city, the thought of all those lines edging forward, was too much with us, and we started to wander again. A minor errand (made work, really) took us down to Astor Place, and we passed Cooper Union, shut tight, its Great Hall closed. We stopped to read a plaque commemorating the appearance there of Lincoln, not yet nominated, in 1860. He had come East in a new, ill-fitting broadcloth suit to plead, with eloquence and hard facts, the cause of the Union. Lincoln, we thought, would have been comforted by the long lines at the many polling places, and by the solemn faces of the people. One thought leads to another (work was now out of the question), and we strolled uptown, past lines in front of schools, churches, and shops, and into the American Wing of the Metropolitan. Our thoughts stretched ahead into the future, but we wanted to touch the past. We walked through the proud old rooms from Ipswich, and King George County, in Virginia, and Albany, and looked at the bright handmade silver, the Gilbert Stuarts, the mantelpieces, and the gleaming gold mirrors surmounted by eagles. Dusk was settling in when we left the Museum, and our path home took us again past those long, silent lines. When the polls closed, we settled down to await the returns.

November 1960

CHAPTER 16

GREAT DAY

OUR MAN STANLEY DROPPED BY the office a day or so after the Johnson Inauguration, remarked, "The nation is in safe hands," and deposited the following dispatch:

"Have been in Washington for Inaugural ceremonies. Arrived on Capitol Hill early on morning of swearing-in, wrapped to ears in red-white-and-blue thermal underwear, protection against predicted frigid weather. Underwear not visible, of course, beneath overcoat, jacket, vest, sweater, scarf, and galoshes. Looked like any other man heavily bundled. Precautions largely unnecessary, since air crisp but not numbing. Sun broke through swiftmoving clouds. Flags everywhere, gaily flapping. Capitol itself all dolled up—massive, gleaming. Scales of Justice on pediment looked newly gilded. Giant loudspeakers emitting recorded Mozart Piano Concerto No. 21 in C, filling huge plaza with beautiful music. Marine Band took places directly in front of and below stand where President due to take oath of office; Mormon Tabernacle Choir took places directly in front of Marine Band.

Mormon Choir warmed up, sang several hymns. 'The hard part is to look good,' said unidentified Mormon voice through loudspeaker. 'The eyes of the world are upon you!' 'Testing. One, two, three,' said unidentified man in gray fedora into microphone on President's podium. All nearby roofs dotted with dark figures of security guards, many precariously perched on high, dangerous places. Mounting excitement as House and Senate arrived, took places in stands on Capitol steps. Supreme Court arrived, took places on Presidential platform. Mrs. Humphrey arrived. Mrs. Johnson arrived, in coat of American Beauty red. Smiled gently at crowd. Mr. Humphrey arrived. Sounds of 'Hail to the Chief' as President moved slowly down broad steps. Dignity of President threw instant hush over crowd. President tall, tanned, purposeful. Ceremonies under way moment or two behind schedule. President stood up to take oath as bells pealed all over city, followed by deep booming of twenty-one-gun salute. President forgot to raise hand until one-third through oath; repeated oath in low voice. Address followed, delivered in slow, almost conversational tone. Crowd seemed deeply moved—listened largely in silence. Then National Anthem played, and ceremonies over. Crowd stood for several minutes watching tall figure of President walk slowly back up steps and into Capitol. Crowd seemed under spell, pondering President's words. After several minutes, crowd suddenly smiled, laughed, talked, moved off Capitol Hill.

"In evening, in Temperate Zone underwear and black tie, to Inaugural Ball at Sheraton-Park Hotel. Ballroom festooned with multicolored garlands of artificial flowers. Flowers everywhere—along sides of yellow-draped boxes, hanging in clusters from ceiling. Peter Duchin, with twenty-two-piece band, elegant at piano, alternated with Count Basie, equally elegant but steamier. Inaugural Ball dispensed favors for women (gold bracelets with tiny medallions picturing President and Vice-President) and for men (silver key chains with medallions). Profusion of pink among women; men in black tie. Spotted numerous heavily pleated dress shirts among men. One aristocrat self-conscious in white tie and tails; fellow had been misinformed, and looked it. Huge colored photostat of painting at one end of ballroom—pictorial representation of song 'America the Beautiful.'

Picture bursting with homely scenes—farmhand driving cow with stick, two small boys seated on hillock watching steam-driven wooden train chug past, two elk chasing each other through tall pines, neatly husbanded farm with grain neatly stacked beside barn, and rugged, snowcapped mountains. As I stood looking at picture, lady with sequined glasses brushed past, wearing tiara composed of letters 'TEXAS' in red, white, and blue. Letters flashed on and off. 'You're from Texas,' I said. 'How did you know?' she said, her head ablaze. 'I use two batteries for this thing, and I've brought a supply of extras,' she said. 'I'll be all right if I don't blow a fuse.' Lady disappeared into throng, her sign blinking. Floor jammed with tall Texans. Texans subdued, affected by occasion. Floor now too crowded to dance on; crowd almost motionless. Count Basie, undaunted, kept up Basie beat. Chief Justice and Mrs. Warren took places in Presidential box, behind Presidential and Vice-Presidential seals. Secretary of Treasury Dillon arrived, Justice Clark arrived, Secretary of Labor Wirtz arrived, Ambassador Adlai Stevenson arrived, Acting Attorney General Katzenbach arrived, all took places in Presidential box. A. Philip Randolph and Ralph Bunche arrived, took places on folding chairs reserved for Medal of Freedom winners, in front of Presidential box. 'We must clear a path for the President and his party!' cried a commanding military voice, and crowd was gently hustled behind golden cordon.

"Long, suffocating wait. Room so crowded everybody's hands pressed to sides. 'I have come to the conclusion,' said distinguished-looking man beside me, 'that the new Sam Rayburn House Office Building can best be described as "aggressive eclectic."' As good a remark as any, under circumstances. Sudden vast applause from far end of ballroom, near grand staircase. Spotlights played over throng, focussed at far end of room. 'He's coming!' said man beside me. At approximately 11:40 P.M., band struck up 'Hail to the Chief.' Band kept striking up 'Hail to the Chief.' Must have played 'Hail to the Chief' half-dozen times. Chief moved slowly down cleared path, smiling, shaking hands. More relaxed than during morning ceremonies but still quiet, immensely dignified. Both Humphreys appeared in Presidential box, followed by First Lady, in Yellow Rose of Texas gown and accompanied by daughters. Daughters enjoying every minute of it. Escorts of daughters clean-cut, embarrassed. President appeared in Presidential box. With superhuman effort, crowd managed to disengage hands from sides, applaud wildly. President sneaked quick glance at wristwatch. Obviously man with long road and many problems ahead. President walked to microphone in box, seemed to shed cares. Was pretty funny for any man at midnight, let alone a President. Made small, informal jokes about Humphrey doing talking this evening while he would do dancing. Said that after four other balls he and Secret Service were happy. Crowd roared. 'One thing you can say for the Great Society,' said President, 'it sure is crowded.' President looked at occupants of box. President greeted 'our great Chief Justice,' introduced Adlai Stevenson, and said, 'Ambassador Stevenson is in charge of making your world better, and he is doing a fine job of it. And now let us dance!' Entering penny-size area cleared for him by Army, Navy, Air Force, Marine Corps, and Pinkerton men, President scooped up Mrs. Johnson and began majestic twirl. President led with firmness, changed partners several times, and, moments after midnight, glanced swiftly at wristwatch again and silently disappeared through rear door, headed for home and the great affairs of state."

January 1965

CHAPTER 17

FIRST NIXON INAUGURAL

Writing about the first Nixon Inaugural, I resorted to a trick, pretending that the report came from a fictitious scholastic, a Dr. Bell. This harmless device threw the bird dogs of the justly famed *New Yorker* checking department into a tailspin. A harried young woman from checking came to my office. She appeared stricken. "We cannot find Dr. Clement Wilson Bell in any reference book, *anywhere,*" she said. "Where in the name of God does this man teach?" I explained the situation. Somewhat satisfied that she would not be held responsible for this alteration of fact, she left my office with the look often seen on a checker's face, a look that seems to be saying, "Writers are crazy. What can you do?"

Looking back, I realize that no one could have predicted Watergate and the whole Nixon saga. Since I am by nature optimistic I take an upbeat attitude toward each of these quadrennial blasts. As I grow older I realize that Bernard Shaw said it all in the title of his wonderful play, *You Never Can Tell.*

WHEN WE HEARD THAT AN old friend of ours, Dr. Clement Wilson Bell, planned to be in Washington at Inauguration time, we asked him to drop us a few informative lines after the festivities. Dr. Bell is a retired professor of comparative civilizations at a small, choice Midwestern college; he is totally detached and nonpartisan, and casts a cold eye. Herewith, his report:

"*Ave!* I have just returned from what you might call a city of masks, and no mask is more compelling than the one assumed by defeated persons departing from public life. Not for them the visible tear, the long face, the hapless slouch. Several days prior to the Inauguration, I found myself a late-afternoon guest in the classical redbrick Georgian house of Robert Kintner, who had been officially close to President Johnson. He had gathered together a stellar group, led by Vice-President Humphrey, who had, as you know, been on the wrong end of the recent returns. Here and there I spotted several Associate Justices of the Supreme Court, exuding permanence and dignity, but for the most part this cheerful, tinkling house was occupied by those going out rather than those staying in. Mr. Humphrey was tanned, ebullient, brisk, and trim as he moved swiftly around the room, a glint in his eye and a spring to his walk. I am not saying that this man was happy. I am saying that he *appeared* happy, and that no shadow of malevolence or envy crossed his face, and I admired the mask, if mask it was. I sat down beside a handsome woman who was wearing a high-rise birdhouse of a hat—a birdhouse with duplex, even triplex apartments. 'Presumably, there is a good deal of moving out, of sad farewells,' I said. 'Moving?' she said. 'Who's moving? We'll sit this one out; we sat out the last one. Nobody's moving except the Katzenbachs and Betty Furness.' She had herself recently received a surprisingly cordial letter from the President-elect, who thanked her for some good wishes he had heard she had expressed in his behalf. 'I puzzled over this,' she said, 'for I fought him hard in the campaign, and then I remembered that I had taken a train ride with an associate of his and had passed some generalities about the rigors of the job, and said that I wished him well. I'm not sure it's his real signature, but I admire his system.'

"Washington can be miserable in the rain, even before so gala an event as an Inauguration. Georgetown—manicured, precise, a bijou—does not lend itself, streaming wet, to elevation of the spirit. Downtown, the huge government buildings melt into square and heavy shadow. In the back streets, gray prominence is given to the row upon row of stooped houses and faceless windows. The people brace themselves against the wind and the rain, and bustle along and betray nothing. They could be in Providence or St. Louis or Denver, trying to stay dry and warm. I wandered into the handsomely restored Ford's Theatre, and was instantly gripped by the melancholy and haunting past. The pert young guide from the National Park Service had done her homework. She had the details at her fingertips. 'The assassin first had a few drinks at a nearby bar to get up his courage, and then sneaked up the main stairs over there, and into the President's box, with his dagger and his derringer,' she said. 'The President and Mrs. Lincoln were side by side, Major Rathbone a few feet away. The assassin fired point-blank, vaulted over the box rail, caught his spurs on the Treasury Guard flag adorning the box, fell to the stage, broke his leg, staggered across the stage and to a waiting horse. He is said to have shouted "*Sic semper . . .* "' And there, indeed, was the empty box, garlanded with flags, and the stage, brilliantly lighted with a replica of the set for 'Our American Cousin.' And below, in a small museum in the basement, a life mask of Lincoln, and the huge shawl that Lincoln wore—bigger than a blanket, bigger than a man.

"I heard there were other real masks—this time of Nixon—at the Hawthorne School, in southwest Washington, where various anti-war and just generally anti-groups were planning what they called Counter-Inaugural ceremonies. More driving rain, and into the lobby of the school, where milling hundreds of young men and women in dungarees and sweaters, many wearing dead-white masks of Nixon, were signing up for seminars and buying anti-literature. The masks sold for one dollar, and people looked less false with them than without them, since their own faces betrayed little emotion. Their expressions were blank and distant. They wandered about. I wandered about. I found myself in a long hallway. Some thirty to forty young men and women were slowly writhing and wriggling and holding out their hands to one another, turning and twisting and groaning. Their faces were masks of passivity. I asked a pleasant young blond-haired chap what was up. 'They are relating to one another,' he said. 'They are reaching out; they are learning their tactile possibilities. Say, are you with the FBI or the CIA?' I let it pass, and moved into a class-room where a seminar on underground media was under way. A young woman instantly approached me, placed a scarf over her mouth, and mumbled, 'Beware. The FBI is in the room.' A booted young woman was expressing her opinion that the mass media were doing their best to destroy the underground press. 'They play us for suckers. They give us hours on their television. They write us up—and all to make freaks of us, to dishonor us. Our job is to produce our own thing and have like nothing to do with them—to spread the word ourselves.' Some people wearing Nixon masks walked past, and nobody knew who anybody else was.

"Still rainy and windy, but I sloshed up to the tent the demonstra-tors had pitched near the Washington Monument, where they planned a Counter-Inaugural Ball. The rain had turned the ground into thick brown mud, with so powerful a grip that it almost sucked off my shoes. I had lost track of time now, and the tent was filled with closely packed young people—several thousand together in one place but not together in any other sense—responding to a speaker's denunciation of United Fruit. The boos that greeted mention of the words 'United Fruit' were spiritless and seemed to mask a deeper discontent. The voice from the platform grew more urgent. There were housekeeping problems now. Shoes and stockings were caked with mud. A voice, through a bullhorn, said, 'Chick Norick, please meet Katy O'Donnell at the front.'

"Dark now, and I left the tent and walked past the brightly lighted Washington Monument. I could see the Capitol (lighted) at one end of the city and the Lincoln Memorial (lighted) at the other. And as I walked past the Statler Hilton, pondering the reaching out and the tactile relating, there was a great flurry of motorcycles, and sirens, and revolving red lights, and the President-elect swept out of the drive-way, trying to communicate with a small knot of people gathered on the street, his face almost pressed against the window of his limousine as he waved and waved again, and then he was gone, and his wife's golden coiffure was clearly visible through the rear window of the car. The lobby of the Statler Hilton was all silks and satins and fur pieces, with everyone wandering around, on the way to a party or from a party, or not even going to a party, and most of the wanderers with expressions that betrayed no feelings. The White Tower across the street was warmer in spirit. There was a sense of skill here, a wonderment that the dark-skinned lady in charge of the sizzling grill knew precisely what she was doing every single moment with her patties of meat. She seemed to have three hands, four hands, five hands, and they flashed and moved and picked up buns and poured cheese onto meat and put meat into buns and buns onto plates, and handled the french fries and drew the coffee, and she never changed her expression but got on with her work. She smiled only once, at a particularly skillful maneuver with a bun. A bedraggled girl holding on to a wall telephone watched her, wide-eyed. An elderly woman watched her, wide-eyed. Two young girls wearing pink hair bows and little signs on their white dresses reading 'Friends of the Nixon Family' watched her, wide-eyed. She was doing-her-job, and she was doing it expertly.

"The next day, the rain let up, and I found myself at the swearing-in ceremonies on Capitol Hill, seated next to Mayor Lindsay, of your city—a charming man, with a beaver hat, who told me that he, like me, had put on thermal underwear for the event. 'We have sent a hundred and thirty police down here. Costing the city thirty thousand dollars. They'll march today.' Mrs. Lindsay was deep in *The New York Times*. Someone called out to the Mayor, 'Writing up the Inauguration for the *Village Voice*?' 'I've got a program of my own,' he replied. The thousands massed in front of the place where the oath was to be taken watched the officials on the platform and closely scrutinized Huntley and Brinkley and Cronkite in their heated salons on the tall television-and-camera tower facing the podium. Huntley and Brinkley watched the people. Security men watched everyone, their eyes slowly moving from clump of persons to clump of persons—down, up, across, down, up, across. There were no expressions on the faces of the security men, and no expressions on the faces of the television men in the tower above, and no expressions on the faces of the crowd. All masks were A-O.K., all set to go. There was no expression on the face of the leader of the Marine Corps Band. The dignitaries trooped to the front of the podium. Mr. Billy Graham was masked in a high-bronze-tone makeup that gave him the appearance of a traveling Cherokee performer. A slight expression broke through the mask of Mr. Johnson—a quizzical, slit-eyed expression. Mr. Humphrey's gay mask had gone, disappeared, and had been replaced by a thoughtful, bemused one, as though he were almost blindly staring at a Chinese scroll being unrolled backward. Mr. Agnew an enigma, Mrs. Nixon an enigma, but very strong and erect, and Mr. Nixon evidently trying to break through the mask in time for his moment of transition. During the swearing in and during the Inaugural Address, the barriers between himself and the people in front of him did seem to go down. The President-elect was now the President. The role was now his. He was playing his part well, and he appeared to be enjoying it."

February 1969

CHAPTER 18

HAND ON CARDOZO

A WORD ABOUT JUDICIAL MEDIOCRITY versus judicial excellence. A week or so ago, Senator Roman L. Hruska, of Nebraska, felt compelled to answer the charges of mediocrity brought against Judge G. Harrold Carswell, President Nixon's nominee to the Supreme Court of the United States, by remarking, "Even if he were mediocre, there are a lot of mediocre judges and people and lawyers, and they are entitled to a little representation, aren't they? We can't have all Brandeises, Frankfurters, and Cardozos." This reminded us of some words written by Judge Learned Hand, himself one of the supreme jurists of our time (and a man who did not suffer mediocrities gladly), in appreciation of Benjamin Cardozo, shortly after Justice Cardozo's death, in 1938. We would like to share those words in these strange times:

In all this I have not told you what qualities made it possible for him to find just that compromise between the letter and the spirit that so constantly guided him to safety. I have not told you, because I do not know. It was wisdom: and like most wisdom, his ran beyond the reasons which he gave for it. And what is wisdom—that gift of God which the great prophets of his race exalted? I do not know; like you, I know it when I see it, but I cannot tell of what it is composed. One ingredient I think I do know: the wise man is the detached man. By that I mean more than detached from his grosser interests—his advancement and his gain. Many of us can be that—I dare to believe that most judges can be, and are. I am thinking of something far more subtly interfused. Our convictions, our outlook, the whole makeup of our thinking, which we cannot help bringing to the decision of every question, is the creature of our past; and into our past have been woven all sorts of frustrated ambitions with their envies, and of hopes of preferment with their corruptions, which, long since forgotten, still determine our conclusions. A wise man is one exempt from the handicap of such a past; he is a runner stripped for the race; he can weigh the conflicting factors of his problem without always finding himself in one scale or the other. Cardozo was such a man; his gentle nature had in it no acquisitiveness; he did not use himself as a measure of value; the secret of his humor—a precious gift that he did not wear upon his sleeve—lay in his ability to get outside of himself, and look back. Yet from this self-effacement came a power greater than the power of him who ruleth a city. He was wise because his spirit was uncontaminated, because he knew no violence, or hatred, or envy, or jealousy, or ill will. I believe that it was this purity that chiefly made him the judge we so much revere; more than his learning, his acuteness, and his fabulous industry. In this America of ours where the passion for publicity is a disease, and where swarms of foolish, tawdry moths dash with rapture into its consuming fire, it was a rare good fortune that brought to such eminence a man so reserved, so unassuming, so retiring, so gracious to high and low, and so serene. He is gone, and while the west is still lighted with his radiance, it is well for us to pause and take count of our own coarser selves. He has a lesson to teach us if we care to stop and learn; a lesson quite at variance with most that we practice, and much that we profess.

April 1970

CHAPTER 19

MASS IN TIME OF WAR

By the time of Nixon's second Inaugural, my customary optimism was shattered. The Vietnam War had split the country apart. A sense of despair had spread through the land. My report itself had a strange, despairing history. Mr. Shawn instantly bought it, set it into type, but he never ran it. He told me many times, and with feeling, how much he liked the piece, but each time he spoke he had an odd look on his face. He would not explain why the piece did not see the light of day. A good friend of mine in the magazine's legal department, lowering his voice as though we were being observed by Big Brother, said to me one day, "Outside forces somehow have objected to this piece. Don't ask me any questions because I can't give you any answers." The manuscript itself is in the Manuscripts and Archives Division of The New York Public Library, along with other *New Yorker* papers (many other things of mine are in the Philip Hamburger Papers of the same division) and there it sits, as puzzled as the author.

HISTORY, TOO, IS INSTANT NOW. I went down to Washington for the second Inauguration of Richard M. Nixon and attendant events just a few weeks ago, but they have already become in my mind part of some ancient, dreamlike pageant in which the characters are not quite real, and acted out their parts in some distant historical past. I was swept almost within minutes of arriving in Washington to the Lincoln Memorial—a restorative rewarding place to check in. Home ties are reestablished; faith is renewed. The ceaseless war in Vietnam had not yet ceased. Lyndon Johnson was still alive; flags flew at half-mast in honor of President Truman. Washington was having a spell of unseasonably mild, springlike weather, but there was ice on the reflecting pool in front of the Memorial. There was a steady stream of hatless and coatless people—mostly young—climbing the long white stairs to the Memorial, and standing, as they always do, for long moments in front of the solemn, kindly figure. I moved over to the north wall to read again the words carved there from his second inaugural: "With malice toward none, with charity for all . . ." I went down the stairs, facing the Washington Monument in the middle distance, encircled by a ring of flags, with the Capitol directly behind, sitting solidly on Capitol Hill. There were only three days until the Inauguration, but the city itself was quiet, without any noticeable air of anticipation. Hotel lobbies had not yet crowded up. The Inaugural stands had been constructed along Pennsylvania Avenue, and bunting was displayed in front of many stores. The new subway under construction lent the downtown area a chopped-up, improvised appearance—gaping holes, huge machinery, thick wooden planks over the streets, and the deep echoing rumble of cars passing over the planks. Here and there, I spied unexpected bits of street life: lovely open-air flower and fruit stalls, jewelry put on display by young street vendors, many of them selling peace emblems—peace signs dangling from necklaces and on rings. But there were hurried, fleeting glances from passersby, and few smiles. An immense, overbearing truck, garishly painted in red, white, and blue, its horn honking madly, came careening down K Street, asking all the world to make way and bearing the sign "Excavation Construction Company."

I spent a quiet evening with friends at a quiet house in the residential Northwest section. There were pewter candlesticks on the dining-room table, and discreet hunting prints on the walls. All those present were connected, on various levels of the bureaucracy, with the government. Wives were on hand. The men appeared to have resigned themselves to the glacierlike movements of the bureaucracy, and I detected a wry detachment, as though they were visitors in a strange land, observing the strange customs with equanimity and poise. World-shaking events are going on all around us, they seemed to be saying, but the pageant is a continuous one, and since the script is almost always the same, it doesn't really matter when one takes one's seat or when one leaves. A young man poured himself a spot of brandy. He worked in a "sensitive" area. "I hear that the President brooks no opposition," he said. "People just don't say him nay. The Democrats are told nothing, but the Republicans are told nothing, either." He sipped his drink. "People down here don't much question the motives of a President; we don't ask as many questions as out-of-town people do; we don't bother with that. Actually, it's considered bad form to discuss politics in the bureaucracy. It would be like touching on a man's religion." An elderly man cut in. "Actually, we aren't much bothered by Presidents," he said. "We engage in very little speculation about them; we take a relatively even-tempered view of them. The machinery continues to function. I guess that's one of the troubles." Some of the ladies present were impatiently concerned with peace and its prospects. As far as the men were concerned, the war had apparently become part of the bureaucracy. And, in a sense, was subject to the self-imposed ban of *politesse*. One older man, who was connected with governmental science matters, seemed disturbed. He refilled his bourbon glass. "I have been taken quite aback by the President's letting his science adviser resign, and apparently abolishing the post." He said, "The adviser himself had behaved with great caution. He made no false moves. It is a matter of immense importance to have a science man in the White House. For one thing, someone should be there for immediate advice in the event, say, of a power failure, or mercury poisoning, or a fuel-oil crisis—someone others can work through, can have confidence in. I still feel that the nation wants the comfort of believing that its brainpower will be put to use. Now if you want some information, I'm told, you will have to go through the Secretary of Agriculture, and cut through layer upon layer of the bureaucracy." A man who had served in posts all over the world was impatient with strident critics of the United States, who felt free to tell the United States how to conduct its business without paying sufficient attention to the motes in its own eyes. "I am not quarreling with that," said the man with the bourbon, "but the fact is that if you ask an awkward question these days of the Administration, you are met by a tight-lipped silence. They suddenly get formal. They say they'll get back to you. And they never return a phone call. It certainly looks like a new Administration, and he has certainly telegraphed his moves. He's engaging in a form of colonizing—moving people who have been trained for four years in the Executive Office of the President out to the various departments. It's a proconsul arrangement. For one thing, this President has no ties to the bureaucracy, and secondly he has strong beliefs in big-business management techniques. The secrecy makes everybody feel cut off—Congress, the press, people. Now, obviously, every bureaucrat feels that the fat is in the other fellow's budget, but matters have become formalized, and a sort of adversary procedure has developed. What really surprises me"—he stared for a long time at his drink—"is that Mr. Nixon didn't explain the Hanoi bombings." "What surprised me," said his wife, "was the bombing itself."

I drove back early and caught a glimpse of the Potomac and Roslyn, across the river in Virginia, with its brightly lighted clusters of new high-rises and motels, a twinkling, almost alien colony in contrast to the staid, low-lying capital. It was ten o'clock, and Washington had apparently gone to bed. The streets around the White House were deserted. The simple white-porticoed St. John's Church, on Lafayette Park, was dark. The Tayloe-Cameron House was dark, the Cutts Madison House was dark. Andrew Jackson, on his horse in the middle of Lafayette Park—"as archaic as a Ninevite king [as Henry James once remarked] prancing and rocking through the ages"—was bathed in a sweet-and-sour orange glow from huge lights spread around the park, and illuminating not only Jackson but massive trucks parked in the park and spread out at jaunty angles to one another. They contained intricate cable and television equipment for the televising of the Inaugural Parade, which would pass in front of the reviewing stand in front of the White House, directly behind the park. They gave the impression that the circus had come to town and bedded down. Here and there, along the Avenue, there were scattered sounds of hammering from workmen putting finishing touches on the stands and caught in the strange orange glow. I walked over to Pennsylvania Avenue and the color scheme abruptly changed. The White House was bathed in the whitest, cruelest white lights I have ever seen. They were lights without compromise, and they set the house off by itself. This is the *White* House. The President lives *here*.

Two days before the Inauguration, I went out Connecticut Avenue for a talk with Jerry Gordon, national coordinator of the National Peace Action Coalition. He was planning a big march for Inaugural Day. Mr. Gordon, a veteran of many peaceful marches and demonstrations, was not permitting his energies to flag. His various offices and assorted warrens were scattered throughout the DuPont Building, in the heart of the bombed-out subway area. Mr. Gordon indulges in a great deal of walking, and he does a considerable amount of his thinking while walking. To avoid wasting time, his wife prepares sandwiches, which he manages to nibble while traveling throughout the DuPont Building. I was told that if he wasn't on the fifth floor, he might be found on the twelfth and if not on the twelfth, then perhaps the fifth again, or, better still, the eleventh. He was somewhere, and he was busy. I finally caught up with him on the twelfth, but we soon shifted to the eleventh. Mr. Gordon is a serious and dedicated man, with a look of perpetual concern. The offices had an atmosphere of controlled but vigorous activity. There was a purposeful air, but nothing frenetic, and no jingling of telephones. Gordon thought that the Christmas raids had sickened and traumatized people. People who had never before interested themselves in protest had now volunteered. There was a general sense of revulsion. Middle-aged and older people had particularly stepped forward. There had been many calls from smaller cities that had never showed much interest before the Christmas bombings. Five hundred and forty new names had been added to their lists. Fifty-five cities were sending buses into the District of Columbia. "I sense that the feeling of hopelessness is going away," he said. "There is bitterness, and a sense of deception, and an overriding desire to influence events. All these combined have created a compulsion to bring people into the streets on Inauguration Day. We are getting splendid cooperation from the District police—electric generators, backup sound equipment, carefully worked-out lines of march, and disciplined training for peace marshals. One can no longer call this a youth movement, that's for sure." Three people converged on Gordon, commanding his attention. "When peace happens, peace will happen," said the elevator man as I rode down. "We'll see."

My first official event—which took place later that day—was the reception for the Vice-President at the Smithsonian Museum of History and Technology. The event was by invitation only, and apparently thousands had been invited. Scores of buses were lined up outside the museum waiting to disgorge their passengers. Washington was emerging into a sort of Inaugural life now. Traffic was coming alive all over town, filling the streets and snarling them. Downtown Washington had begun to bulge under the pressure of events, and had produced a paralysis that is *sui generis*. The paralysis is felt all down the line. In Washington, it is symbolized by the distinct, highly audible, and totally unrestrained use of police whistles. Police were everywhere around the Smithsonian, blowing their whistles. They blew and blew. The whistles were shrill, high, and piercing. Occasionally they were blown in one long terrifying sound. More often, the pattern was three or four rapid, tense blows. Washington was filled with the sound of them. The official guidebook to the Inaugural had suggested that the women wear afternoon dress and gloves; gentlemen, business suits. But the major problem was to reach the Smithsonian. The ladies, many of whom seemed to me to be overly done up, waited patiently in the buses for the doors to open, while what I took to be elderly drill sergeants, replete with medals, made an attempt to direct traffic. "No one leaves these buses until I give the direct command order," a short, muscular, uniformed man barked at a covey of women who were about to step down from a bus. Somewhat terrified, they fell back. "No one moves until I give the order," barked the putative sergeant.

The ladies were in no mood to question authority. They had conquered Phase One of the problem: they had reached the building, or
its vicinity. Actually getting inside took time, and the line stretched
from the curb to the doorway and moved slowly. Outside the rear
door, a hatless and coatless middle-aged man was passing out leaflets
titled "Why Vietnam?" It chronicled events beginning with the first
Indochina War in 1858 and running through America's increasing
involvement. There were few takers. People stood patiently in line,
ignoring the man. Once the doors themselves had been reached, a display of credentials was required, and the women's handbags were
peeked into—an act performed with dispatch and courtesy by the
Secret Service. A more serious problem now presented itself. Where
was the Vice-President? There was an intense crush on all floors.

"I think he's on the first floor," said a guard, "but there's at least a
two-hour waiting line."

"He's resting," said another guard.

"I think he has gone home," said a third.

"I have come all the way from Little Rock," said a lady with a
battleship-gray choker. "Don't tell me I can't find out what floor
he's on."

When it became apparent that only a tiny few of the surging,
milling crowd would catch even a glimpse of the Vice-President, the
crowd fell into a lesser diversion: The Pursuit of the Plastic Glass.

"You must get a plastic glass," a lady whispered to me.

"Why?" I said.

"*Why* the plastic glass?" she said. "They are to become the No. 1
souvenir of this Inaugural. They are designed like champagne glasses,
with narrow stems and small bases, and they have embossed on them
in blue a seal that says "The Inauguration of the President and the
Vice-President. They are *invaluable*. My sister has managed to get
hold of seven of them."

"Why are you waiting in this line" [we seemed to have fallen into a
line], I asked, "if your sister has seven of the glasses?"

"I want some for myself," she said. "Besides, at the end of this line
they are serving domestic champagne and Tropicana juice. Optional,
one or the other, and then you just dry the glass and take it home."

I finally made it to some Tropicana juice, nibbled at a corn muffin, and carried my dry glass away with me.

Next day, I drifted over briefly to the neighborhood of the Corcoran Gallery, for a second official event: Salute to America's Heritage. This was to be a tribute to America's "ethnics," and the Inaugural Guidebook advised, "Casual dress; coats and ties not necessary." A dismal, driving rain had set in, and a long line of patient, gray-looking people wound solemnly around outside of the gallery. Inside, one had been promised samples of food that was light-years removed from Mom's apple pie. New gastronomic vistas were to be opened up, and with them, it was hoped, new understandings of ways other than our own: bitterballen, galantine of pheasant, stuffed grape leaves, pork-stuffed cabbage, guacamole—that sort of thing. I stood in line for one hour in the rain and listened to the mad birdcalls from the police whistles, and the line barely moved. At one point, I shuffled past an exit from the Corcoran, and saw an elderly lady in a wheelchair who had evidently been rushed out into an alleyway and was being administered oxygen.

"Last night at the Salute to the States," said a man behind me, "I heard Bob Hope, and he was real nice."

A lady next to him smiled. "I thought it was real nice when Governor Wallace couldn't stand up, and the crowd stood up for him."

"I closed a deal with a man from Tennessee for half a million dollars," said a man from under a dripping umbrella. "Real estate. I'm from Indiana."

The line still had a long, long way to go. We inched past another exit door from which people were stumbling forth into the rain.

"Don't go in!" cried a man who was emerging. He looked completely exhausted. "It takes twenty-eight minutes just to get across the floor, and you can't see a single blessed thing."

A lady stopped by to warn the line to forget it and go home. "You'll never make it inside *today*," she said, "and if by some miracle you do, you might run across a pickled herring."

A florid, middle-aged man emerged from the exit, carrying a plastic glass. "It's worthwhile!" he cried.

The morning before the Inaugural itself, I went out to the

Washington Cathedral, and had some coffee with Francis B. Sayre, Jr., the Dean of the Cathedral, who had offered to turn over his church that evening to a Concert for Peace. Leonard Bernstein, an orchestra, a chorus, and soloists were to perform Haydn's *"Missa in Tempore Bello"* ("Mass in Time of War"). The President himself planned to attend an inaugural concert by the Philadelphia Orchestra, conducted by Eugene Ormandy. The Dean received me in his study, a quiet room with mullioned windows. He is tall and long-jawed, and, as has often been remarked, bears a resemblance to his grandfather, Woodrow Wilson. He was dressed in black clericals, and he clasped and unclasped his hands. He walked back and forth with big strides, and the room seemed almost too small for him. He speaks in soft tones, and his smile is warm. "The concert we will hold here tonight," he said, "is in no sense a 'counter' concert. The word 'counter' is out. That's not the idea at all. (To the coffee table for a cup of coffee, then back to the window.) The concert will be done in the spirit of dissent. Dissent is proper—it's part of our country. I don't think any single mind started the idea of the Mass. Some twenty peace groups asked to use the Cathedral. Abigail and Gene McCarthy wanted a rally. I said no. No rally. No speechmaking. Martin Peretz, of Harvard, said to me, 'What about a peace concert?' I liked the idea, and I called Bernstein, and he agreed, and plans were formulated. The music will say it. The music will say it all." The Dean moved slowly back and forth across the room. "I don't know what I'm going to preach on Sunday," he said, and I had the impression that he was not marshalling thoughts just for the moment. "What the war has done, really, is pull off the mask," he said slowly. "The mask was pulled away and the hollow substructure, there all along, became apparent. And now we have to face the moral problem. There it is, clear and plain. We have nothing to be responsible to. We have no criteria, nothing to rally to. Where is the consensus to which one can turn? Not in the agencies of government, not in the universities. They are unguided. Where is the shared feeling, the common faith? The Vietnam War has been anarchy, and the moral anarchy is everywhere in the world today. There was considerable moral ignorance in the Second World War. I took a survey of ethical concerns during that war and was appalled at the results. A few Lutherans showed up. On my own ship, in the Navy, I handled matters by simple, plain decency. But what did we do as a nation? We sold our ideals down the river. We went in for colonialism. Don't misunderstand me—there is still a great reservoir of ethical concern. There is still a huge iceberg of moral probity, but it is melting. Somehow, it must be mobilized. We have dealt with everything except the ethical problems. I have hope in our indigenous and creative spirit. What is revealing can also be healing. I think we are saying *mea culpa* to ourselves right now. We are repentant. We are turning inward. Peace marches are fine, a passion for freedom is fine, but certainly it is not enough merely to say 'Peace! Love!' Where will they come from, where will we find them?" He fell silent for quite some time, with his hands clasped behind his back. "I feel that God is wiser than I am," he said. Then he turned slowly and faced me. "What we need," he said, "is a kinship with a forgiving God."

Looking back now, from the vantage point of a cease-fire, it is difficult to imagine the intensity of emotion in and around the Cathedral that night. Lines began to form at four in the afternoon and became ever longer. The Cathedral sits on high sloping ground, and its square Gothic tower dominates its sector of Northwest Washington. As darkness came over the city, the tower itself became illuminated in a soft and restful light. The temperature dropped considerably. An icy wind blew. Heavy rain fell. The lines wound down and around and around the church. They were hushed. Many of the people had wrapped themselves in blankets against the biting wind and rain. And still the lines got longer. The atmosphere of pilgrimage and dedication was unmistakable. By seven-thirty, when the Cathedral doors opened, officials estimated that close to ten thousand people were waiting to get in. The Cathedral can ordinarily accommodate twenty-five hundred people. On great occasions, such as this one, a form of ecclesiastical stretching is employed. A genial, gently booming voice, coming from nowhere through loudspeakers, explained that people had been handed numbered tickets outside the Cathedral and would be allowed inside in blocs. "Fifteen hundred will come in from one side," said the voice. "Fifteen hundred from the other." From time to time, the voice called out various numbers. "Numbers 292 to 667—for the transepts," said the voice. "Numbers 668 to 1094." I walked up twisty, narrow medieval stone stairs and took a seat high in the north transept, an aerial perch that looked down far below upon the marble floor directly in front of the high altar. Above me were massed flags, a gossamer railing, and thin pillars. The crowd moved in noiselessly. "We are approaching the Cathedral's capacity," said the voice. "Now standees on the west, now phase four on the south, and now you must prepare to share the outdoors." A stir went through the crowd as Ambassador Averill Harriman, his tall frame slightly bent, walked to a reserved seat. A giant wave of applause—unexpected under the circumstances—greeted Senator Kennedy and his family, and the audience craned to catch a glimpse of them. Bach, Mozart, and Scarlatti pealed forth from the Cathedral's organ, and the Cathedral seemed to tremble.

Shortly after nine, Dean Sayre, in white vestments now, slowly mounted the high altar. The private figure, quietly probing his thoughts a few hours before, had now become a public figure, imposing and distant, and was playing his role in the pageant I was viewing. The audience was still. "The yearning for peace has brought us all here on this rainy night," said the Dean. "Way down deep is the longing for peace. We were meant to live in peace." He prayed:

> Mend, Lord, the brokenness of mankind;
> Our brutal blindness, the willful lack of care.
> Heal the angry wounds we anonymously inflict upon each other.
> Grant us more than momentary respite from the gory dance;
> But rather that we may know the deeper patience of a brother's love,
> And see the shadow of Thy holiness
> Writ upon each human face —
> Brown and yellow,
> and white,
> and black —
> masked now by the agony
> of man.

Former Senator McCarthy made a few remarks. Then the chorus and soloists entered; Leonard Bernstein, in his dark blue suit and a red tie, entered; and the Mass began. Bernstein was at his gravest. The music lasted for an hour. The audience sat almost motionless. The words cut deep, and with the last notes of the Agnus Dei—"O Lamb of God that takest away the sins of the world, grant us Thy peace"— there was a collective sigh, as though people had been holding their breath for this moment. As the crowd filed out, the voice of the loud-speaker spoke once again. "And a safe journey home," it said.

Part of the beauty of the Inaugural ceremony itself on the Capitol steps consists in the lack of surprises. This is a drama that America knows by heart. The lack of surprises represents continuity, the orderly flow of government in a democratic society. Almost to a man, the weather predictors called the wrong turn. "Balmy weather," they had said. "A spring gambol. Highs in the sixties." And so on. Actually, there was a driving wind, with a sharp cutting edge, and temperatures were in the thirties and low forties. Scarves, mittens, thermal under-wear, and thermos bottles of hot coffee were highly desirable Inau-gural gear, and only a few came equipped with them. On Inaugural Day, Washington traffic becomes truly tangled. Traffic up and down Pennsylvania Avenue, for example, ceases at 10 A.M., and the prudent tend to arrive early. I was among the prudent. I had my thermals, and I had my credentials, cleared by the Secret Service, to seats in the lower stands directly in front of the spot where the President and Vice-President would take the oaths of office. To reach this area, one had not only to flash a small white card, but to pass scrutiny by many exceedingly sharp eyed men, whose glances either took in my whole person by starting at my head and running down to my shoes, or, in the case of some agents, starting at the shoes and running to the top of my head.

Everything proceeded according to schedule. The Marine Band was on hand for martial tunes. The seats in front of the Capitol slowly filled up. The celebrated television commentators arrived and took their places in their elevated booths, facing the lectern. I caught a glimpse of Henry Cabot Lodge, waving. I caught a glimpse of Colonel Sanders, waving. There were numerous benedictions and prayers. Choruses from the combined service academies sang "America the Beautiful." Members of the Senate and the House arrived, moving down the front steps and taking their posts to the right and left of the lectern. Senator Javits was hatless. Senator Jackson waved a great deal. After more than an hour and a half, down the steps came the families of the President and the Vice-President—Mrs. Nixon in turquoise, Tricia Nixon Cox in raspberry tweed with a blue-fox muff, Julie Nixon Eisenhower in apricot, and Mamie Eisenhower in flaming red. "Hail to the Chief" and "Ruffles and Flourishes," and in a moment both the President and the Vice-President had been sworn in by the Chief Justice. Mrs. Nixon kept her eyes closed much of the time. The President delivered his Inaugural Address in a quiet voice. "In our own lives," he said, "let each of us ask—not just what will the government do for me but what I can do for myself?" And the second term was under way. The ceremonies closed with the singing of "The Star-Spangled Banner" by Ethel Ennis, a black singer from Baltimore. Miss Ennis contributed one touch of surprise. She changed the rhythm of the old song, rocked it, cajoled it, put soul into it. The President never took his eyes from her. Small and remote on the podium, surrounded by the massive weight of all three branches of government, she seemed to be saying, "I will be heard."

By nightfall, the city had seen the Inaugural parade and had watched the peace marchers in various parts of town, but mostly on the windswept grounds of the Washington Monument. The grounds were churned up by clumps of mud. Police cars and mounted police were at the base of the monument. By the time the elaborate floats had passed the White House (a few short blocks away) and Father Philip Berrigan, his trenchcoat buttoned up against the chill, had addressed the last remnants of the peace turnout, an exhausted, spent quiet settled over the city. The peace marchers had taken down their placards and headed home.

Nightfall also brought the Inaugural Balls—a prime ritual in the Inaugural ceremonies. People pay forty dollars a ticket, and as high as one thousand dollars for a stall, which is called a box. Men wear black tie (or white), and the ladies wear long gowns suitable for a "ball." The words "Inaugural Ball" evoke gentility, amenity, grace, as well as a certain lifting of the spirits, a bravura send-off to one's leaders, but Inaugural Balls have increasingly become massive traffic jams, both within and without the halls. I arrived shortly after nine at the

Smithsonian Museum of History and Technology (the particular ball to which I held a ticket), and mobs were already surging through the doors. A ball at the Smithsonian holds certain advantages. Although I knew that sooner or later I would be reduced to standing absolutely still, face forward, unable to move either forward, sidewise, or backward, I also knew that with a bit of luck I might examine scattered exhibits of general interest and kill some time before the President and his family arrived. Those same old sharp-eyed chaps were at the door—glance up, glance down, glance across. "There's a hatcheck facility on this floor," said an amiable man, "but I think you will do better on the second floor." I faced a Model T Ford, which stood just below an elegant seal that read "Inauguration of the President and Vice-President." It was the seal that embellished the coveted plastic glasses. To one side, in a cabinet, were a tire pump, a duster, and a pair of goggles suitable for motoring. A large photographic blowup of Henry Ford seated in some tall grass and looking bucolic dominated a wall. "Ladies, we must look in your purses, thank you, thank you," said the plainclothes guards, and the ladies, their dresses swishing, opened their purses for inspection. "At least a thirty-minute wait for hat-and-coat checking on this floor!" said a uniformed guard. The escalators beckoned. They moved at a fast clip, bearing hundreds upon hundreds of people to upper floors at what seemed to be inordinate speed. On the second floor, the hatcheck people said it was hopeless. Not a chance for a hat or coat to be checked. It might be hours. Even months. "In fact," said one official, "we just simply aren't checking anything anymore." It was suggested that it would be better just to carry the coats over one's arm—a first for Inaugural Balls. As in the case of the Vice-President's reception, no one knew whether the President was coming, when he was coming, or where he would show up if he did. Thousands milled about. Bands played. There were scattered bars—four drinks for six dollars, six drinks for nine dollars—and the crowds around them were clumped and disorganized. Everybody seemed to be wandering. There was a look of mounting horror on people's faces. Many of them had come long distances, with finery, and at great expense, and here they were shuffling up and down narrow corridors past iron toys—express and gravel trucks, fire engines, milk wagons, ice wagons, water-powered spinning frames, early patent models, gas engines, ornamented owls, and cigar-store Indians. The American past was spread out before them, was all around them, and they were circling it aimlessly, because there was nothing else to do at the Inaugural Ball. I stood a long time in front of a toy circus: a tiny figure was balancing himself on his hands. There was a Ferris wheel. An antique merry-go-round went round and round. The crowds kept pushing through from behind, and I found myself in front of an immense iron horse—the John Bull engine, which ran on the Camden and Amboy Rail Road from 1831 to 1865. Many people were clasping the plastic souvenir glasses. "I have six of them," a woman called out. "Four in my purse, and two in George's inside pocket."

The crowd was growing larger. There was hardly an inch in which to move. I found myself in a large exhibit chamber with model rooms from the White House, and inside the glass-enclosed rooms were eerie, almost lifelike figures of past First Ladies in their Inaugural gowns, a strange, silent assemblage of the wives of the Presidents. Ellen Axson Wilson was wearing soft velvet brocaded in a design of roses. Helen Herron Taft was wearing a high waistline with a long clinging skirt and a long train. Edith Kermit Roosevelt was in a brocade of heavy robin's-egg blue, Frances Folsom Cleveland was in iridescent taffeta brocaded with a design of black overlay. They were peaceful-looking women, many of them long gone, and, like many women that night, all dressed up and no place to go.

I spied a corridor on the first floor where Secretary of State Rogers was holding court from one of the boxes—stalls with narrow rails, and covered with a simple buff material. Further along this corridor was another huge seal identical with the one on the plastic glasses. Something was going to happen here, I said to myself; this is the place. Ray Block and his orchestra were playing on a platform directly beneath the seal, and an energetic singer attached to his group endlessly twirled and twirled, snapped her fingers, and cried "Hotcha! Hotcha!" Out of the corner of my left eye, I spied Barbara Walters in a brightly lighted booth. We were jammed solid now. There was no moving in any direction. Many black people were in the crowd. There were many children and many old people. The singer twirled and sang "Hotcha!" The band played "When the Saints Go Marching In." The band played "Some Enchanted Evening."

A woman behind me kicked another woman.

"You cut that out," said the woman who had been kicked. "There was simply no excuse for that."

"Ladies! Ladies!" cried a man on crutches. "Patience!"

"I see Kissinger," said a man behind me. "He's in the booth with Ed Newman." I stood on tiptoes to catch a glimpse of him, but by then he had darted out.

"I must push my way out of this," said a young woman in front of me. "I swear I am going to faint." Eventually, she pushed her way somehow to the edge of the throng and through a small door, closed to the public, marked "18th and 19th Century Clocks."

I stood and waited, helplessly penned in. There were hours of this. A great cheer suddenly went up. Someone important was coming through, and in a flash the Vice-President was on the platform directly before us. The crowd made a disappointed but respectful sound. "Don't think," said the Vice-President, with an air of rugged geniality, "that I didn't hear that groan. I heard that groan. I understand that groan. You thought the President was coming." He beamed at the crowd for a moment or two. He then praised the President. He said that there was nothing he could possibly say about the President that could do the man justice. He became quite serious. One could see that he was not a man to be trifled with, even at a ball. "When we have peace," he said, "it will be a peace that will last for a long time. And it will not be a peace of surrender, or the peace urged by people who followed the enemy's propaganda line. It will be the peace of our great President!" This brought an immense cheer but little clapping, since nobody could dislodge his hands. The Vice-President was gone as rapidly as he had come. A long wait again. A wait of at least two hours. Many people had fainted. Others took deep breaths, and floated as best they could, held up by the support of surrounding bodies.

"I don't think he'll ever come," said a woman in blue satin.

"Sooner or later, we'll all have to go home," said another woman.

"Patience," said the man on crutches. "There is no way out, anyway."

Suddenly, spotlights were turned on. An expectant shout went through the almost numbed crowd. Stony-faced men appeared at far-away doorways. There was a great wild cheer and a craning of necks and people standing on tiptoes, and there, on the platform, was Richard M. Nixon. He smiled and bobbed from side to side. He waved his family up on the stage behind him. Mrs. Nixon had changed to her Inaugural gown now—silver lamé and turquoise-blue organza with diamond-and-pearl-like embroidery traced in silver threads. She smiled and held her head to one side in a proud way. And Tricia and Tricia's husband, Eddie Cox, looked quite pale after the long day. The President seemed to have shed many of his cares. He was in a master-of-ceremonies mood. "I apologize for keeping you all waiting for so long," he said. "But you must remember that I waited eight years for an Inaugural Ball. *(Laughter)* I think *this* ball is largely composed of people from the East. *(Cheers)* I have nothing against the East. I think there are people here from New York *(Cheers)*, from New Jersey *(Cheers)*, and from Connecticut *(Cheers)*." The President was warming up. He smiled and moved his hands around in a chopping motion. "Oklahoma!" someone called out from the rear. "Oklahoma!" said the President with mock seriousness. "I hear Oklahoma all over the place tonight at all the balls. They must be everywhere *(Cheers)*. I don't even have anything against Massachusetts. I don't." *(Laughter)* His face became stern, almost severe. "I have seen analyses of the election that prove that I made more gains on a percentage basis in Massachusetts *than in any other state!*" *(Laughter and applause)* A smile once again crossed his face. "No, I have nothing against Massachusetts, " he said. "Julie went to college there. And Eddie went to Harvard there. And he survived!" *(Wild laughter)* "And I don't have anything against New York. Tricia was married in New York, and Eddie passed his bars there. And not the sort of bars you have been passing this evening!" *(Wild laughter)* The

President asked for everybody's help in the days that lay ahead, and was then swept out through a side door by the Secret Service men. It was past one o'clock in the morning of the second day of his second term as President of the United States.

The next afternoon, I went on a guided tour of the city in a tourist bus. One stop was at the Arlington Cemetery. "There is enough coffee served in the Pentagon in one month to float the biggest battleship in the world," the guide said as we arrived. "We have clear visibility today. The cemetery is certainly picturesque. Arlington will be completely filled up by 1980."

February 1973

CHAPTER 20

CARTER INAUGURATION

OUR INAUGURAL CORRESPONDENT, apple-cheeked and frost-bitten after attending the recent ceremonies in the nation's capital, has sent us the following dispatch:

Clear, clean, shining white ice everywhere, and bright-blue sky above. The weather set the tone: one had to bundle up, keep warm, press forward. I arrived in Washington a few days before the actual Inauguration, and pressed forward. Bleachers for the Inaugural Parade were still being put together near the Treasury Building and the White House. Lafayette Square, across from the White House, was a tangled trailer camp of immense television-cable vans. Finishing touches were being put on the reviewing stand where the new President would sit and watch the parade. A flag flew from the top of the White House: the outgoing President was still in residence. The white of the White House glowed. The White House lawns were snow-white, Capitol Hill was snow-white. The city was crowding up—endless buses, hawkers, balloons, Carter buttons, Ford buttons, tiny gold-plated peanut pins (brisk demand). A distinct air of courtesy, expectancy, general good manners. Literally hundreds of events, most of them free. I went off to see "Treasures of Tutankhamun" at the National Gallery, and fell in with a delegation of the wives of mayors (reflected local power) and a pride of schoolchildren. Old King Tut (he was really young, and died early) exercised temporal power briefly thirty-three hundred years ago, and crowds gathered around the cabinet containing the gold-and-blue striped crook and the flail that he carried on certain state occasions. Symbols of mighty power, now in a Plexiglas case. A teacher said to her charges, "Have you thought about how old some of these things are, and how delicate?," and the class nodded, in a bewildered way.

I did a good deal of skipping around. I skipped down behind the White House to the frozen Ellipse, where the Tempel Lipizzan Stallions were to make a wintry appearance. A gallant, frozen band of people awaited the horses, but a genuinely saddened man announced that the horses had unanimously nixed the scheme. Too cold, too slippery. Skipped over to the National Portrait Gallery, in the Old Patent Office Building—a Greek Revival gem once described by Walt Whitman as "the noblest of Washington buildings"—and saw its current show, "Abroad in America: Visitors to the New Nation, 1776–1914." Amidst the massive peacefulness and great elegance of the building, quotations from distinguished visitors to American shores caught my eye, including Harriet Martineau's "I regard the American people as a great embryo poet: now moody, now wild.... There is the strongest hope of a nation that is capable of being possessed with an idea." The past swept up and over, and I walked through the stately Lincoln Gallery, where his second Inaugural Ball had taken place, and through high-ceilinged rooms now hung with American art.

Two nights before the Inauguration, an increasing excitement in the streets. Bitter, near-zero weather for the fireworks near the Washington Monument. Thousands of people around the Ellipse were seated in their cars, windows tightly closed, waiting for the extravagant display. I braved the cold, and stood with scattered knots of enthusiastic people, some in bluejeans, some encased in sleeping bags.

The show lasted a full half hour—fountains, skyrockets, gerbs, flowerpots, wheels—to the accompaniment of band music. Here and there, people yelled "Hooray!" in the clear, cold night. There were guards in all the small guardhouses behind the fence of the White House, and they seemed to be cozily minding their business, and staying warm. Birds were talking in the magnolia trees behind the White House, cold or no cold. They were determined to say what they wanted to say. A guard suddenly came around the outside of the fence and directed his flashlight at the thick White House bushes. Nobody there. No danger tonight.

One day before the Inauguration. The doorman at the hotel complained that his earmuffs didn't fit him properly. In short, his ears were cold. Went off to the reception for the Mondales at the Old Pension Building—high-roofed, massive, designed by General Montgomery C. Meigs in the eighteen-eighties, and once called Meigs' Old Red Barn. But fashions change and Presidents change, and the old Italian Palazzo-cum-Victorian-style building is now overwhelming, with its interior court two hundred and ninety-two feet long and its Corinthian columns one hundred and fifty-nine feet high. Cleveland's Inaugural Ball, held there on March 4, 1885, was the first since the Civil War to be attended by great numbers of Southerners. The imposing pillars were originally painted to look like Siena marble. Mr. and Mrs. Mondale—direct, friendly, at ease—stood in a receiving line just below the Air Force Strolling Strings. They greeted everybody who stepped up, and what seemed like thousands stepped up. Spotted Averell Harriman in a greatcoat, looking trim, tanned, and young. Spotted Treasury Secretary-designate Michael Blumenthal, Peter Rodino, Al Shanker. Noted Georgia fruitcakes, strawberries, watercress sandwiches, Joan Mondale's pumpkin bread, drinks. Mondale was in a sober dark-blue suit and dark tie, and spoke of his hopes for a close working relationship with Congress and for reunifying the nation behind principles that had made the nation great. We were all getting into the spirit now. I went down to the Library of Congress cafeteria for some fried chicken. Later, after dusk, I went to the Longworth House Office Building, on Capitol Hill, for a party of the Georgia State Society, held in the cafeteria of that building—low ceiling, stainless-steel equipment, pipes, coffee urns, the cafeteria décor enlivened by lots of balloons and bunting and puffs of colored paper. The Georgians were happy, and they were gracious. They were being entertained by a four-piece combo—the Gran Jazz, of Griffin, Georgia. Met a Mr. M. Yoshida, whose card, instantly offered, identified him as executive vice-president of YKK Zipper (U.S.A.), Inc., with offices in Lyndhurst, New Jersey, and two hundred and fifty employees in Macon, Georgia. He said that when Carter was Governor of Georgia he had encouraged Japanese investment there as part of his trade program. Mr. Yoshida was pleased with Carter; he was also pleased with the zipper business. Yummy things at the Georgia State party: spiced shrimp, crab salad, sides of beef, rare. Back onto glazed streets. House and Senate office buildings brightly lighted, corridors mobbed, hundreds of people pouring through to one party or another. Slid over to Library of Congress, and to the free concert, in the Coolidge Auditorium, of the Western Wind Vocal Ensemble (under Inaugural auspices), singing songs from the singing schools of the Revolutionary and Federal periods. Hall jammed—scores of young people carrying knapsacks. Left Library of Congress, wondered about transportation, and was hailed by a quiet woman in a station wagon, who said, "Hop in. It's too cold to walk. I'll take you where you want to go." Took advantage of her hospitality and asked if she would drive past Blair House. Carter had arrived a few hours earlier and was in residence there. Not a soul outside Blair House, but an imposing man stood squarely behind the glass front door, his arms crossed, guarding the President-elect. But there didn't seem to be much danger that night, either.

Inauguration Day. Bright sky again, but the temperature up a bit. Still a great chill in the air. Stopped off at a drugstore at Seventeenth and K Streets shortly after 9 A.M. and was told by an excited clerk that if I would just wait a moment John Wayne would be right back to pick up a prescription. Said I had to hurry along to the Capitol and watch the swearing in of a new President. Took a stunning subway, with soft lights and orange-and-beige seats, on an almost noiseless ride to Union Station. Military guards everywhere, examining credentials, but politeness, soft speaking, and smiles were the order of the day on Capitol Hill. Marines were in dress uniform, and the one who took my ticket had no overcoat—his teeth chattered. Sat down just below the stand where the President was to take the oath, and glanced at the vast crowd that had already filled the East Plaza on Capitol Hill and was backed up all the way to the steps of the Senate office buildings and the Supreme Court. Senators and representatives filed in and took their places to right and left of the Inaugural platform. The United States Marine Band was massed below and in front of the platform, and in front of the Marine Band was a hundred-and-twenty-four-voice all-black choir, both men and women—the Atlanta University Center Chorus, led by Dr. Wendell P. Whalum. The crowd was very quiet while assembling, but there was something unmistakably emotional in the air. Some of the emotion burst through when the choir sang "The Battle Hymn of the Republic." President-elect Carter took the oath. When he paid his unexpected tribute to his predecessor, an unknown young lady seated next to me apologized for some tears trickling down her cheeks. They quickly froze. When President Carter said, so softly that it could barely be heard, "We are a strong nation and we will maintain strength so sufficient that it need not be proven in combat—a quiet strength based not merely on the size of an arsenal but on the nobility of ideas," the "special" people on the platform and directly in front made no stir, but from the anonymous crowds far back came a roaring wave of applause. He had been heard back there.

President Carter's and Mrs. Carter's long, steady outdoor stride down Pennsylvania Avenue, the cries of "He's walking! He's walking!," the Carters' brief and relaxed-looking appearances at the Inaugural Parties (formerly Balls)—I hold these in my mind. But I also hold some words that Oliver Wendell Holmes spoke in 1913, at a dinner of the Harvard Law School Association of New York: "It was evening. I was walking homeward on Pennsylvania Avenue near the Treasury, and as I looked beyond Sherman's statue to the west the sky was aflame with scarlet and crimson from the setting sun. But, like the note of downfall in Wagner's opera, below the skyline there came from little globes the pallid discord of the electric lights. And I thought to myself the Götterdämmerung will end, and from those globes clustered like evil eggs will come the new masters of the sky. It is like the time in which we live. But then I remembered the faith that I partly have expressed, faith in a universe not measured by our fears, a universe that has thought and more than thought inside of it, and as I gazed, after the sunset and above the electric lights there shone the stars."

February 1977

CHAPTER 21

FIRST REAGAN INAUGURATION

OUR SPECIAL INAUGURATION CORRESPONDENT, having taken a few days to separate the various strands of what he saw and felt in Washington, has filed the following report:

Funny thing, but when everything happens at once nothing seems to be happening. Curious historical slow motion sets in, which in this case transformed installation of a new President, release of hostages, fireworks, throngs, parades, receptions, and national currents and hopes into an apparently predestined tableau—one that might have been rehearsed for many months. Washington itself was notably subdued during weekend before the ceremonies. Spent quiet evening with old friends in Georgetown, and their minds drifted back to other times and other Presidents. Host said, "I can recall when President Truman asked Dean Acheson to become his Secretary of State. Acheson demurred. He told the President that he didn't feel qualified for the

job. Truman gave him a long look. 'There may be at least fifteen people in this country who could do as good a job as you, but I don't
know their names,' said Truman. 'As for being President, I don't feel
qualified, either, but *I've* got the job.'"

Spent a morning in a high-ceilinged, ornate room in the Senate
Building picking up credentials for the swearing in. Important part of
an Inauguration, since credentials are carefully screened, and Secret
Service must grant clearance. Encountered exceptional courtesy and
good humor on everybody's part. Was handed elegant invitation, seating pass, admission card to the Capitol Building on Inauguration Day,
and two handsome photographs—of Ronald Reagan and George
Bush. Thanked a lovely lady and a hard-eyed Secret Service man, and
wandered through the Capitol corridors. Found myself in room that
served as the Senate Chamber from 1810 to 1859, now elegantly
restored. Thomas Jefferson inaugurated in this room on March 4,
1801. Very quiet, very distinguished chamber, carpeted in red with
gold stars; has numerous shiny brass spittoons near the mahogany
desks, and each desk bears a small nameplate, a white quill pen, a
silver-topped inkwell, and a bottle of blotting sand. Passed through
the old Supreme Court Chamber, with a robe hook for each Justice,
one marked with a white knob reading "The Chief Justice." Washington fever beginning to hit me. Almost hung my hat and coat on the
hooks.

Nearly three o'clock on Saturday now. Walked over to Corcoran
Gallery for opening of Leonardo da Vinci exhibit—the Codex Leicester,
bought in London last December for five million eight hundred thousand dollars by Dr. Armand Hammer. Sedate crowd at Corcoran.
Spotted Dr. Hammer, a spry octogenarian; a very beautiful Kay Halle;
and Paul Volcker, chairman of Federal Reserve. Murmur of excitement as Mrs. Reagan was introduced, to warm applause. She was in
bottle green, and looked stunning. "I am honored to open this
Leonardo exhibit," she said. "My husband and I were in the arts ourselves until we found another line of work." She cut ribbon, formally
opening exhibit. A sumptuous buffet followed. Biggest shrimps I have
ever seen. Biggest shrimp *dip* I have ever seen. Smoked salmon being
sliced with Renaissance delicacy. Everywhere, a multitude of crudités,

all being discreetly gobbled up, to accompaniment of discreet music from string orchestra at bottom of grand staircase. Codex, in Leonardo's own hand, consists of seventy-two sheets, ingeniously displayed separately, so that one can see both sides of the manuscript, written backward in brown ink in Renaissance Italian. My knowledge of Renaissance Italian skimpy, and I had no mirror, so took everything on faith. Leonardo, I learned from printed legends beside the manuscript pages, dwelt in spare yet eloquent detail on water currents, astronomy, geology, and other matters. He wrote that he gathered ideas and observations as they occurred to him. He explained that "air must have darkness beyond it, and hence it appears blue," and went on to say that "the Reader will not wonder if I make great jumps from one subject to another."

At six o'clock, fireworks, at Lincoln Memorial. Have rarely been so cold. Feet and hands had no discernible connection with other parts of body. Memorial floodlit in the crisp evening air. Huge throng walking briskly toward monument. In roadways, almost total gridlock. Crawled over miles and miles of television cable and took up post in front of monument at moment Mr. and Mrs. Reagan started slowly down the broad marble steps. Could see Old Abe in his marble chair behind them, inside monument. Abe hatless. Reagan hatless but wearing heavy dark overcoat and striking white gloves. Mrs. Reagan looked as cold as everybody else. Both Reagans took places at foot of steps, and blankets were placed over their knees. Reagan extremely alert to everything—especially to playing of "The Battle Hymn of the Republic." Fireworks beyond one's childhood dreams: the whole night filled with bombs bursting in air, rockets, shooting stars. Hundreds of big bangs. Seemed as though entire city were under attack. Offered silent prayer of thanks that the brightly lighted sky and the explosions all around were peaceful demonstrations. People standing near me had small transistor sets: no word on hostages yet. Reagan left without speaking but with a broad wave of the hand.

Next day, traffic at absolute standstill. Tried to take cab down near White House but abandoned it blocks away and walked past Blair House and White House. Huge crowds standing outside watching limousines come and go. Very orderly air, no tension. Police very calm. Walked down to Corcoran again, this time to see the exquisite

Nigerian terra-cotta heads from the fifteenth century, and was surprised to find huge crowd, mostly black parents with their children, many of the children perched on parents' shoulders. A quiet, intense experience, and the look of pride on the faces of the onlookers something not to be forgotten.

Monday afternoon, and events began to pile up. The Vice-President's Reception at the Museum of American History was expected to receive fifteen thousand visitors. Most of them, it seemed, were lined up patiently outside museum, moving ahead barely at all along Fourteenth Street and down Constitution Avenue in order to reach long, tunnel-like yellow canopies leading up to the museum itself. Figured these people might be there for hours, even days. Thanks to credentials, was able to take up post looking into the well of the Foucault Pendulum—showing the earth's rotation—a floor below me. Red-coated color guard on a platform, with silver pikes. One redcoat carried a huge, old-fashioned painted drum. Military everywhere in dress uniforms. Again, a great throng, as Bush was to make several appearances during afternoon and people were being admitted in shifts. "I try to take in as many historic events as possible," said lady standing beside me with two small children. "I take the children everywhere when there is a historic event. At the Dallas Fair, I lost my little boy in the crush. Tom thought I had him, and I thought Tom had him, and it was a *mess*." There was a sudden hush. Mr. Bush bounded onto platform, followed by Mrs. Bush. Great applause. Bush boyish, exuberant, said he had been observing Mr. Reagan closely the last few days. Said he was in a position to do so, and he wanted each and every one of us to know that Mr. Reagan was anxious to get on with the job, to perform the work for which he had been elected. "And you all know what I mean by that," he said, to tumultuous cheers. I glanced down at pendulum below me and noticed a sign on railing which read, "Although the pendulum seems to be rotating slowly, actually it is you and the museum that are rotating."

Tuesday—Inauguration Day. Down to swearing in by subway. Profound courtesy in Washington from the subway set toward strangers. People patiently explain intricacies of how to obtain fare cards, make change, and insert cards, and tell you what station to step off at. Smooth, lovely subway. Transistor radios in great profusion now. Hostages still not free. Thousands and thousands in subway, but no shoving or other rudeness. Damn hard to believe. Washington subways are deep under the earth, and the escalators at one of main exit stations for the ceremony—Capitol South—were not running, so thousands trudged up many steep stairs clasping their portable radios. Walked with throng toward the West Front of the Capitol. Had choice seat beneath platform, next to spirited California woman who was wearing large button depicting Ronald Reagan in a cowboy hat. "You would make me extremely happy if you would wear a Reagan button," she said to me, producing a small gold-plated pin reading simply "Ronald Reagan." I accepted pin. "This whole thing," she said, with a broad sweep of her hands, "is a tribute to what the country now thinks of California. Bringing in people like Sinatra, Carson, and Hope. That's what California can do. Those are the most important people in the country, and they are California-based." She said she had not bought a new dress specially for the occasion; she was wearing short brown boots and a cloth coat trimmed with fur. All around us, however, were ladies wearing mink and sable and occasionally ermine. Small children scattered everywhere displayed large quantities of photographic equipment—cameras and telescopic lenses.

Solemn ceremonies got under way with the Marine Band playing everything from Sousa to Gershwin.

"Some of those people up there behind the dignitaries," said the lady beside me, "are Eagles."

"Eagles?" I asked.

"Eagles," she said. "Eagles give ten thousand dollars per annum to the Republican Party."

"Per annum?" I asked.

"Per annum," she said.

I turned around in my seat to catch a glimpse of the huge mass of people stretching out behind me toward the Mall.

Both Houses of Congress arrived. The Supreme Court arrived. "Leonine," muttered a man next to me, referring to the Chief Justice.

The diplomatic corps arrived. "They're not out yet," said someone in my row. "Almost, but not quite."

Mrs. Reagan and Mrs. Carter took their seats. Jimmy Carter

entered, and "Hail to the Chief" was played for the last time in his Presidency. Reagan was delayed coming through the rotunda of the Capitol to the platform. Then he arrived, to the accompaniment of a mighty trumpet flourish. Carter looked composed, and had a warm smile on his face. Reagan was solemn and dignified, and took the oath of office with deep emphasis on every word, every syllable. "I do solemnly swear that I will faithfully. . ." A peaceful transfer of power, and half a world away another transfer of power was within grasp. When Reagan finished his speech, it was his turn to be greeted with "Hail to the Chief."

The thousands slowly filed from their seats toward the broad avenues of the city. It seemed that everybody now had a small radio.

"I think they are airborne!" shouted someone in the crowd.

"I don't think they have cleared Iranian air space!" called out another.

I had a brief lunch in the Senate Refectory (the traditional Navy bean soup) and walked onto the East Front to watch the President join the parade. "They are really on their way home now," said a guard on the Capitol steps. He was clearly moved. The President emerged briskly from the Capitol, in his morning coat, and entered the open rear seat of his limousine. The First Lady, in a red twill cavalry coat, stood beside him. He looked years younger than when he had delivered his Inaugural speech, only an hour or so before. The huge plaza outside the Capitol was cleared of everybody but dignitaries and police and motorcycles and Secret Service and special guests. The cavalcade started down Capitol Hill onto Pennsylvania Avenue, and headed toward the White House.

As for me, I walked and walked. In the evening, in a crowded, silent bar on Pennsylvania Avenue, I watched the hostages emerge from their plane at Algiers, and then I walked over behind the White House to the Ellipse and stood a while in front of the now fully lighted Christmas tree behind the South Lawn. The words "And crown thy good with brotherhood from sea to shining sea" kept running through my head. We could do worse than hold on to the thought.

February 1981

CHAPTER 22

WE HAVE NOTHING
TO FEAR...

FIFTY YEARS AGO, on March 4, 1933, Franklin Delano Roosevelt was inaugurated President of the United States for the first time, and I was there, in the crowd. (This was the last of the March 4th Inaugurations; ever since, they have taken place on January 20th.) I was eighteen, and I drove from college in Baltimore to Washington in a battered Ford owned by a classmate; the mere fact that he owned a four-wheeled vehicle gave him the appearance of being exceedingly rich. The times were desperate. Thirteen million Americans were out of work (including my own father); thousands of families were living in makeshift shacks in our greatest cities; farmers were rioting to prevent foreclosure of their land and homes; hunger was commonplace; and every bank in the nation was about to be closed. I was lucky: I had a scholarship that credited so many hours of work in the library against so much tuition. I was young and healthy and had my share of dreams.

The day was ominously overcast, and became more so as we approached Washington, forty miles south. Thick dark clouds hung over us; I was certain it would rain, and rain heavily. We had no tickets or credentials. The idea was to get as close as possible to the Capitol's East Front, within sight of the Inaugural stand, and find a citizen's perch for the ceremonies. My friend at the wheel knew nothing of the complexities of Washington traffic, and we drove around the city's circles and broad boulevards trying to find a place to park. Soldiers and policemen were everywhere; flags and bunting hung from every lamppost. But there was no hint of festivity in the air. Small knots of people had begun to line the sidewalks (it was late morning), but for the most part they appeared dispirited and sullen. We parked not very far from the Capitol, on a quiet, tree-lined street with neat, clean row houses with white stoops. It was a poor, black neighborhood. I was dressed for the day in the clothes of the time: a dark-blue vested suit (no jeans, of course), a long dark winter overcoat, and a snappy gray fedora with a huge brim. (The suit, as I recall, was a hideous shade of blue, and had come with two pairs of pants, for thirty-two dollars.) In my pocket I carried binoculars.

We worked our way fairly close to the Capitol before being stopped by a Marine guard. With extreme amiability, he asked for our tickets. He then gave us a friendly wink and pointed at a nearby icicle-laden, leafless tree. My friend and I scrambled into the tree and surveyed the special nexus of the nation that spread out before us. The white dome of the Capitol was gray, partly obscured by wisps of fog. The official grandstand was filling up with top-hatted dignitaries, all bundled up against the expected downpour. There must have been a hundred thousand people spread out over the vast Capitol grounds. For the first time, I examined my neighbors in our particular tree, each on a separate bare limb: an elderly gentleman in rumpled and ancient green tweeds, with patches; a beautiful redheaded young woman wrapped in a skimpy coat of rabbit, or of some other unfortunate domestic animal; a woman of indeterminate age who can best be described as dressed in rags, and whose face was lined with worry and pain. For the moment, at least, we were precariously snug in our tree house, waiting for a President to be inaugurated. President or no President, I had a hard time taking my eyes off the redhead; we subsequently became close friends.

The ceremonies were scheduled to start at noon. Noon came and went. The crowd was strangely silent. One could sense the unease. Rumors began to spread through the crowd, called up to the tree people by the less fortunate groundlings. Rumor: A mob somewhere along Pennsylvania Avenue had broken through police lines and surrounded the car containing President Hoover and President-elect Roosevelt. Rumor: Machine guns had been spotted along the route of the cavalcade from the White House to the Capitol. Rumor: Roosevelt had been wounded by an assassin's bullet, perhaps fatally. The lady in rags prayed quietly in the tree: "No more trouble, please, God. No more trouble." The man in the patched tweeds said that he had known all along that something terrible was going to happen on this day, and that one man's leaving office and another man's taking over would have no effect: only revolution would turn things right side up, once and for all. Nonsense, said the redhead; have a little faith, and don't fall out of the tree. Suddenly, there was a stirring in the crowd. The red-coated Marine band directly in front of the grandstand began to play. I pulled out my binoculars and focused straight ahead. President Hoover, glum and downcast, appeared and took a seat in a leather armchair to the left of the rostrum. A sound like the rustling of otherworldly leaves went through the crowd. Far away, through the giant center doors of the Capitol, appeared the President-elect. His face was totally without color. He made his way, painfully and slowly, along the ramp leading to the rostrum, leaning heavily on the arm of his son James. He seemed to be drawing on bottomless reservoirs of physical and mental strength to make the short journey to the rostrum and the Presidency. The crowd held its collective breath. I doubt whether anybody, at that moment, knew that he was carrying ten pounds of heavy steel around his crippled and wasted legs.

I spotted the white-bearded Chief Justice, Charles Evans Hughes. He was wearing an odd black skullcap. As he delivered the oath of office, Roosevelt repeated every word of it in frighteningly solemn tones. Once power had passed into his hands, he seized it kinetically, with a vigor and force that stunned the throng. Both hands firmly gripped the rostrum. "This is preeminently the time to speak the truth, the whole truth, frankly and boldly," he said, in a clear and unforgettable voice. "This great Nation will endure as it has endured, will revive and will prosper. So, first of all, let me assert my firm belief that the only thing we have to fear is fear itself—nameless, unreasoning, unjustified terror which paralyzes needed efforts to convert retreat into advance. In every dark hour of our national life a leadership of frankness and vigor has met with that understanding and support of the people themselves which is essential to victory. . . . Yet our distress comes from no failure of substance. We are stricken by no plague of locusts. . . . Plenty is at our doorstep, but a generous use of it languishes in the very sight of the supply. Primarily this is because rulers of the exchange of mankind's goods have failed through their own stubbornness and their own incompetence, have admitted their failure, and have abdicated. . . . The money changers have fled from their high seats in the temple of our civilization. We may now restore that temple to the ancient truths. . . . Happiness lies not in the mere possession of money; it lies in the joy of achievement, in the thrill of creative effort. . . . Restoration calls, however, not for changes in ethics alone. This Nation asks for action, and action now. Our greatest primary task is to put people to work. This is no unsolvable problem if we face it wisely and courageously. . . . We do not distrust the future of essential democracy. The people of the United States have not failed. . . . They have asked for discipline and direction under leadership. They have made me the present instrument of their wishes. In the spirit of the gift, I take it."

The crowd had come to life. It shouted approval. Roosevelt, still holding tightly to the rostrum, gave no sign of satisfaction. His expression was as grim as when he had started to speak. The ceremony was over. "I think we'll live," said the redhead as we climbed down from the tree. The man in tweeds burst into tears. "You know something?" said my college friend. "It never rained."

For many years, I have kept a tattered bulletin board in the kitchen, every inch covered with tacked-up addresses, memos, cards from loved ones, stray quotations from Shakespeare and Yeats (life-sustaining forces). Among them is an old, pockmarked newspaper photograph of FDR leaning on a cane and listening intently to two ragged men who appear to have stopped him somewhere. I have no idea where the picture came from, but it is one of my priceless treasures. One of the men is small and scrappy-looking. His hands are in his pockets, and he is leaning into Roosevelt's face. The other man, larger and older, is wearing an ancient greatcoat, and is unshaved. Roosevelt's gray hat is somewhat smashed. He is being attentive to every word that is being said to him. The caption reads, "He knew how to listen."

Since that far-off Inauguration, I have learned that the family Bible on which Franklin Roosevelt took the oath of office lay open to the thirteenth chapter of I Corinthians—to "And now abideth faith, hope, charity, these three; but the greatest of these is charity."

March 1983

CHAPTER 23

QUADRENNIAL

JUST WHEN WE THOUGHT we had missed the Inauguration, our man Stanley, an old and avid hand at national ceremony, unexpectedly turned up in our office and deposited the following dispatch:

Have attended Bush Inauguration. Wouldn't think of staying away. This my thirteenth Inauguration, despite personal disinclination for public life. Arrived in Washington several days before swearing in, laden with precautionary long drawers, galoshes, wool sweaters. Weather uncommonly warm, almost springlike, so checked in to hotel near White House, changed to lighter clothing, and sallied forth. City strangely subdued. Bunting everywhere, but few indications of heightened spirits. No possible quarrel with signs displayed by homeless denizens of Lafayette Square: "Thou Shalt Not Kill," "Blessed Are the Peacemakers," "Wanted: Wisdom and Honesty."

Down to Capitol for credentials. Hundreds of people passing through airport-type security, then swarming down seemingly endless corridors, apparently headed nowhere. Picked up gilded invitations to swearing in from old friend Roy L. McGhee, superintendent of Senate periodical gallery, and joined throng of rubberneckers in corridors. Noticed marks on columns in Statuary Hall where pages scratched their initials ("G.F." "M.A. Hill"), saw carved marble tobacco leaves and corncobs on capitals of columns (reminder of early days), passed group of young men wearing Kent State sweatshirts (latter-day history), passed Rembrandt Peale portrait of G. Washington ("That picture alone is worth seven million dollars," said guard), ate fortifying bowl of white-bean soup, and headed for National Archives. Always try to visit Archives. Sense of history, roots. Small but solemn crowd examining original Declaration of Independence, Constitution, and Bill of Rights in "shrine cases," filled with preserving helium. Those documents are heart of the matter. All signatures now badly faded except for a dim John Hancock. Hope he's fully insured, wherever he is.

Pre-swearing-in days something of a blur, since Inaugural events—personal, gustatory, ritualistic, cultural—blend into one another. Had dinner with Washington insiders generally satisfied with state of affairs: amid tinkle of different-shaped glasses, approval of deregulation, free-market forces, relatively hard line on foreign affairs. Grillroom of hotel bubbling with gathering of veterans of submarine crew that rescued George Bush when his TBF Avenger was shot down in Pacific during Second World War. Handsome elderly men, voluble wives. All had been received that afternoon by President-elect and Mrs. Bush in Blair House. Overflow of excitement, as many had not seen one another in more than forty years. "I wouldn't be alive today if it hadn't been for you," Bush said. No eats for them at Blair House, just photo opportunity; supper was being prepared for battalions of grandchildren.

Hotel lobby filling up with assorted elegances. "Damn, there's marmalade all over my credit cards," heard man tell concierge. Invited to elegant reception at National Gallery of Art, given by Ford Motor Company and museum, for viewing of Paolo Veronese show. Museum in happy mood. String quartet. Fountains. Lavish spread of goodies. Spotted Chief Justice Rehnquist, Justice Byron White, Lynda Johnson Robb, and Sarah Booth Conroy, longtime *Washington Post* journalist—kind that doesn't talk, writes. Spoke with ebullient J. Carter Brown, director of National Gallery. "Inaugurations are festive times," said Brown. "And since Veronese is festive this is most appropriate." Walked through Veronese galleries in company of Beverly Brown (no relation), enthusiastic, scholarly coordinating curator of exhibit. Not much about old Paolo unknown to Ms. Brown. "Some of these colors seem to step right out into the rooms," she said, and she was right. "Some of the paintings were on the backs of organ shutters in cathedrals. One must be alert with Veronese. See that horizontal angel floating like a helicopter? He's dropping dates to another angel, and to the side another angel is hanging out the wash."

Swearing-In Day. City still quiet. This transition almost noiseless. My hotel window overlooking 1816 yellow-walled, classic-columned St. John's Church, where Bush scheduled to attend prayer service before start of big day. Secret Service, police everywhere. Shouts from Secret Service to occupants of hotel: "Close that window! Close that window!" No monkey business on *this* street. Rector, resplendent in Episcopal garb, awaiting Bushes in front of church. Suddenly, red lights flash, motorcycles, long black car flying flags, open Secret Service car, ambulance slide up in front of church. Mrs. Bush out one side of car, Mr. Bush out other side. Rector gets kiss from Mrs. Bush, handshake from Mr. Bush. When Bushes emerge from church, short cleric in purple tugs at Mrs. Bush's arm. She turns, gives him kiss. Bushes back in car and heading for White House farewell with Reagans.

Brisk walk up Capitol Hill to West Front. Immense throng attending ceremony. Thousands and thousands, seated, standing, perching in trees. Another security check, and directed to seat directly beneath podium and a whisper away from Marine Band, resplendent in red. Gratified to see women in band. Brisk wind blew sheet music from band into my lap. Returned music promptly, received profuse thanks. Crisis averted. Felt I had played part in march of events. Senators filing in above me. Garrulous, clubby lot. Senator Leahy a camera buff, snapping everything. Kennedy *very* leonine. Cranston in heavy winter coat. Long drawers? Simpson, of Wyoming, immensely tall, obviously big kidder, devoted to high jinks. Stately old ceremony three minutes late. Quayle, having been sworn in first, was thus President for three minutes. Sudden, piercing cold wind. Bush spoke almost conversationally, drew most applause when he physically reached out hand to members of Congress, asking cooperation.

Headed for parade, and got close-up view of President and Mrs. Bush in reviewing stand directly opposite. President took coat off in stand, put it back on. Constantly surrounded by hordes of small children. Mrs. Bush seemed to be running private day-care center on Pennsylvania Avenue. Uncle Sam came past on float. Bush looked tired, Mrs. Bush hyperalert. Wonderful big brass bands letting out all stops as they passed by President. Practically every drum marked "Yamaha." Problem for our trade representative? Replica of TBF Avenger came by. President appeared deeply moved, fondled a pride of grandchildren.

Dusk, and black-tie ball at Union Station. Immense crush. Spied white hair of Mrs. Bush twirling in dance with President in center of vaulted great hall of renovated station. Band played "I Could Have Danced All Night." Bushes danced a few seconds, took off for other crushes. Saw Judge Bork, caught immobile in crowd. "I contributed one hundred thousand dollars," said man standing next to me, his hands pinned to sides. People straggling through train concourse with luggage and no connection with festivities. Electronic monitor announced Executive Sleeper for New York departing Gate C14 at 10:20. On Time. Wrestled way through crowd and took cab to lighted open, colonnaded Jefferson Memorial, on Tidal Basin. Spot almost deserted. Stood and admired nineteen-foot-tall bronze statue of Jefferson facing, in distance, South Portico of lighted White House. Enjoyed notion of third man in office welcoming forty-first to old house across Tidal Basin. Some familiar quotations from Jefferson inscribed on inner walls of memorial. Found self especially moved by "I am not an advocate for frequent changes in laws and constitutions. But laws and institutions must go hand in hand with the progress of the human mind."

February 1989

CHAPTER 24

ONE MAN'S VOTE

ALL THROUGH THE INTENSE Presidential campaign, two lines from *Waiting for Godot* kept running through my mind: Estragon says, "I can't go on like this," and Vladimir replies, "That's what you think." I have voted in fifteen Presidential elections, the first in 1936 (for Franklin Roosevelt, of course), but never before have I or those near and dear reached such heights of pre-election anxiety. Rightly or wrongly, we felt that if our man lost, our country would be lost, too—Supreme Court, jobs, racial reconciliation, abortion rights, you name it. (Even had Hoover been reelected in dark 1932, we would have kept in the White House a President who had appointed Charles Evans Hughes and Benjamin Cardozo to the Supreme Court.) Damp hands, poor appetite, short temper—all telltale signs covered by that irritating Teutonic word "angst." I watched the Republican conclave in Houston with a friend and neighbor who was born in Berlin—a scientist of international renown, driven from his native land by primal hatreds. During Pat Buchanan's preliminary tirade, this man sat silent and rigid, but when Buchanan called for a religious war he leaned over, his face ashen, and said, "I see the armbands."

We devoured the papers, hugged the tube. I noted a fascinating development in the technique of the Big Lie: someone would tell a vicious whopper (implying, with no sustaining facts, that Clinton had been buddy-buddy with the K.G.B., say), and then, the next day—or perhaps just hours later—deny that such a statement had been made. Lying about lying, I hope, will turn out to be a political ploy without a future.

There were bright, even encouraging moments, especially when the tube showed us the excited, smiling faces of thousands who had stayed up long past midnight in small towns all over the map to catch glimpses of Clinton and Gore as they came through on the bus. I was reminded of a day in the forties when I left this office and walked over to Broadway and Forty-fourth Street, near the old Astor Hotel, to watch President Truman (the real live one) ride past in an open car. Huge crowds lined the streets. Truman wore a smile of profound inner confidence. With enormous and unforgettable dignity, he waved to the crowd, and I recall saying to myself, over and over again, "This man connects."

As November drew closer, tension increased geometrically. Daily, we were whipsawed by the polls—it's narrowing, it's widening, it's narrowing, it's widening—and by the ubiquitous pundits. There was a sickening sense that the high office of the Presidency was being demeaned by self-inflicted wounds.

At long last, that memorable Election Day. Teeming rain. At 7:30 A.M., I walked to my usual polling place, to find unprecedented, un-complaining lines. An interminable wait, only to learn that my polling place had been changed to an old-folks' home four blocks from where I stood, dripping wet. Two instant thoughts. One practical: the lines at the old-folks' home would be so long that I should accept fate, throw in the sponge, and prepare to live there. The other, paranoid: the entire election process was a fraud, everybody's venue had been secretly changed, and New Yorkers would be robbed of their votes.

At the home, more long lines, but only three machines. Many citizens, like me, found themselves in an unexpected voting place, and

there was great commotion. "I'm a doctor, and I have patients waiting, but nothing is going to stop me from voting," a young man standing next to me said. "You bet your sweet life," said a businesslike
brunette behind me. "I'm voting today if I have to stay here through
the night." Democracy was rescued by a fragile wisp of a woman, a
volunteer poll-watcher who called herself Connie. Connie had arrived
at six: no officials on hand, no registration books, and one of the three
machines was broken. "I stood on a chair and shouted for calm," she
said. She then methodically reached election headquarters, had the
broken machine repaired, and, clutching a neighborhood list of
addresses, directed people to the proper booths. Finally, I voted. Now
that it's over, my friends and I have not yet unwound. We are smiling
again. Warily.

November 1992

CHAPTER 25

CLINTON INAUGURATION

JUST BACK FROM WASHINGTON AND largest crush of hopeful human-kind in my experience. (This my fourteenth Inauguration, starting with first of Franklin D. Roosevelt, in 1933. Missed only two: FDR's second and third.) Arrived Sunday before Wednesday swearing-in, headed (in mild weather) for huge gathering around Lincoln Memorial Reflecting Pool. Clutched valid invitation to seat near Memorial, for program of pageantry and musical goings on. Fat chance! Thousands upon thousands already there—deep in churned-up mud, lining slippery banks along pool, huddled on quilts and blankets. Many more surging vainly forward, holding equally useless tickets. Had impression *everybody* wearing some sort of button. Buttons of Bill, of Hillary, of White House. Buttons saying "We did it." Thousands of black faces, yellow faces, white faces. No pushing, no shoving. Cynics don't buy this, but there are times when hope is palpable.

Signs everywhere: "First Aid." "Lost Children." Watched small boys scrambling into bare trees for better view of Memorial.

Depth of Depression, first FDR investiture. I'm nineteen, ticketless, facing east façade of Capitol, far away. Spotted leafless tree, climbed branch, shared tree with woman in rags, elderly gentleman in patched tweeds, beautiful redhead. Fitting spot: entire country up tree. Somber, gray, despairing day suddenly electrified by FDR's unforgettable "The only thing we have to fear is fear itself." "I think we'll live," redhead said as we climbed down from citizens' perch. She was right.

Splendid amplification sending forth "Battle Hymn of the Republic." Always showstopper. Booming voice intoning, "And Mr. Lincoln said, 'As I would not be a slave, so I would not be a master.'" Vast crowd fell silent. Voice intoned, "And Mr. Lincoln said, 'Fondly do we hope—fervently do we pray—that this mighty scourge of war may speedily pass away. . . .'"

Stranger beside me said, "I have an unexpected feeling that something good is about to happen to our country."

MONDAY. Breakfast with friend—Thomas H. Allen, former Mayor of Portland, Maine (current member of Portland's City Council). Rhodes Scholar and friend of Clinton's at Oxford. Down for festivities with wife and two daughters. Great admirer of Clinton, especially of his ability—anytime, anyplace—to curl up on bed or sofa, take catnap, regardless of people jabbering, radio blaring in room. "He always woke up refreshed," Allen said. "When he came to Portland last year, he ran us all ragged. He loves reaching out, always asks more questions than are put to him. An immensely serious man, yet full of fun, and an omnivorous reader." Allen particularly remembers the connection Clinton made with the porters at Oxford. "Other scholars were astounded," Allen said. "They would hear porters swapping stories among themselves about the State of Arkansas—anecdotes told to them by Clinton." Allen's first and continuing impression of Clinton: warmth.

Second Reagan Inauguration. Temperature: 4°F. Fear that whole government would freeze to death, nix next four years, turn Reagan into historic icicle. All outdoor festivities cancelled, my lovely ticket invalid. Roy L. McGhee, then Senate Periodical Gallery superintendent, phoned me at hotel, said, "If you can get here in seven minutes, I have a ticket for you inside the Rotunda for the swearing-in." Unforgettable wild ride to Capitol. Fast-talked way past cadres of Secret Service, clock ticking, and was escorted into Rotunda by McGhee just as Reagan, with experienced actor's impressive gait, strode Presidentially into vast vaulted room to take oath.

Treated myself to yummy crab cake (not Baltimore class, but close), and wandered on to America's Reunion on the Mall. Another mob scene. Holiday spirit (it was Martin Luther King Day), with thousands swarming over grounds, in and out of huge white tents featuring music, exhibits, food: fried trout, buffalo burgers, crawfish Monica, chicken Panang. Multicultured bellies. (Maalox moments to come later.) Approached eighty-eight-foot-long wall entirely covered with hundreds of six-inch colored-paper squares. Concept of Brooklyn visual artist Phyllis Yampolsky, who calls it "The American Town Hall Wall." Markers provided, and people scribbling messages, tacking them onto any available space: "Don't Mess with Bill." "One Race: The Human Race." "Sorry to See You Go, George." "Feed the Hungry Help the Homeless Stop the Killing." I grabbed a square of green paper and wrote "Courage!" but before I could reach wall I was tapped on shoulder by Secret Service man, who said, firmly, "Sit down at this table." He then directed a woman and her daughter to sit beside me. Thought for moment we had been mistaken for Iraqi terrorists. "Just keep seated, and don't rise when Mrs. Clinton comes through," said Secret Service man. Moments later, Hillary Clinton arrived, walked past wall, to frenzied cries of "Hillary! Hillary!" Smart. Serene. Long black coat. Stopped by table where I was sitting. Mother beside me took her hand, said quietly, "We need health and education, Mrs. Clinton. Health and education. And don't let anybody fool your husband." Mrs. Clinton heard her. Handed her my green square that said "Courage!" She read it, smiled, looked directly into my eyes, said "Thank you," and was swept along down Mall, trailed by Secret Service men holding thin yellow rope protecting her from crowds.

People again crowded around wall. Un-smiling couple took close look at myriad messages of hope and despair. Man turned to woman and said, "I didn't know there were so many of *them*."

Traffic gridlocked. Cabdrivers unanimous this worst traffic within memory. Kept bumping into friends old and new, many just trying to get across town. Good talk with Haynes Johnson, Pulitzer Prize–winning political writer. He shared my feeling this most important election in sixty years—critical time in nation's history. Said he felt both Justice Department and CIA had become completely politicized, hence vital areas for new administration. Shared my worry about press becoming too aggressive. "I'm worried by a current of cynicism," he said. "An exclusive interview with a high official today would make you appear to be the enemy. If a President calls, you are tainted."

Saw old friend Judy Collins—slim, blue-eyed, excited. All set to sing at one of the balls. Said she'd first met Clintons at Chautauqua in summer of 1991. They had come backstage after hearing her concert. "They evaluate ideas," she said. "They're both so bright, they love good music, they sustain multiple points of view. Artists need support—Clinton seems to understand this." Collins said she hardly believed it when she woke up to find that Clinton had won. She said, "'It was a Chelsea morning, and the first thing that I heard was a song outside my window. . . .'"

Bumped into disgruntled Republican friend. Fine woman, enamored of the likes of William Bennett. Hated Republican Convention, blamed religious right for everything, felt sad to see so many buddies leaving town, and was looking forward to upcoming symposium featuring Cap Weinberger and other disgruntleds. Told her, generally speaking, I was happy that hope springs eternal.

Swearing-In Day. Put on long johns but didn't need them. Cloudless bright-blue sky. Pleased with self for buying Metro ticket ahead: system almost swamped. But, again, no pushing. Unprecedented crowds heading for Capitol. Brisk walk up Capitol Hill. Elaborate security: Secret Service, Marines, electronic checkpoints. Escorted to Seat 53, just below podium. Turned to look back at unending throng far below, stretching onto distant Mall. Official stand behind podium filling up with dignitaries. Marine Band in red dress costume.

> FDR's fourth. Wartime. FDR ailing, in wheelchair, unable or unwilling to make trip to Capitol, sworn in on South Portico of White House. Wind up standing next to Archibald MacLeish, then an Assistant Secretary of State, on narrow balcony of old State Department Building, and catch glimpse of FDR, tiny figure through trees, taking oath of office. MacLeish, in strange gesture, keeps running fingers over engraved calling card he holds. "Feel this," he says to me several times.
>
> Kennedy Inauguration. Bitter, bitter cold. Snow, ice everywhere. Robert Frost solemnly reading poem while smoke curled all around him, lightbulb having ignited speech. Aging poet obviously mistook smoke for cold breath in frigid air, plowed ahead with prosody until alert Secret Service man, aware that the entire United States government was about to go up in flames, somehow extinguished blaze.

Last "Hail to the Chief" for Bush. Somber-faced Clinton took place on podium. Disappointed when Associate Justice Byron White, substituting for Thurgood Marshall, administered Vice-Presidential oath to Gore. At close of oath, White said to Gore, "And I *know* you will." Bandmaster had sharp eye on clock, played rousing medleys until precise second of noon, when Clinton took oath of office. Twenty-one-gun salute sounded through entire city, and nation had new President. Throng moved by historic pageant. Glorious voice of Marilyn Horne, singing of children everywhere. Firm, quiet Inaugural Address (pleased that he said, "There is nothing wrong with America that cannot be cured by what is right with America"). Moved by ending of Maya Angelou's poem:

> Very simply
> With hope—
> Good morning

Lost interest in jam-packed, airless Inaugural Balls years ago. Accepted invitation this time to elegant reception at National Gallery. Chance to see exhibit "The Greek Miracle"—classical sculpture from dawn of democracy, fifth century B.C. Thirty-four objects on display, each a treasure. Nike unbinding her sandal, her beautiful body clearly delineated through flowing sculptural gown. Eerie feeling to stand in front of pieces of stone from, say, 410 B.C. and find them so alive. Listened to audiotape of exhibit, narrated by former director of Gallery, J. Carter Brown, who made clear that besides the aesthetic quality of what stood before us there was another message: In Greek thought, individual was free to take charge of his or her destiny but morally subject to needs of the community. Read in catalogue: "Self-knowledge and social responsibility were civic values that encouraged the development of constitutional democracy."

Something to think about all the way home.

February 1993

CHAPTER 26

POSTSCRIPT:
VERMEER TIME

I AM ONE OF THE LUCKY ONES. I have seen the Vermeer show at the National Gallery in Washington. Forget the numbing circumstances surrounding the Vermeer: museum open, closed; government open, closed; snow. Let's just say that the day I slipped down on the Metroliner the show was open but the rest of the museum was closed. In a stately, pillared court space dotted with chairs and benches on the main floor of the main building, just outside the entrance to the show (a seemingly endless line was being admitted in measured groups), I was greeted by Arthur K. Wheelock Jr., who is the museum's curator of northern baroque paintings and the cocurator of the show. Wheelock, a pleasant, distinguished, passionate Vermeer scholar in his early fifties, has been fascinated by the Dutch master (1632–1675) since long before his graduate studies in art. "I have been totally overwhelmed by the public response," he said. "I suppose it's the mystery surrounding the paintings. Vermeer left no sketches, no drawings. Everything must be learned from the paintings themselves. There's no documentation. For example, everybody has been searching for years for *The Little Street* in Delft. The street itself is nowhere to be found. Once he started to paint, Vermeer altered his own reality. For instance, in *The Little Street* one must look closely at the rust-colored shutter on the door at the right. He *needs* that red shutter, so he alters the width of the wall in contrast to its twin opposite wall. Similarly, in *Lady in Blue Reading a Letter,* you will see a double shadow near the blue chair at the left, a shadow with a deep, rich quality of light that comes from *within,* and not from without—a Vermeer shadow." Vermeer, I gathered, was a man who did things his own way. I was reminded that some years ago, preparing a Profile of the celebrated anatomy teacher and curator Robert Beverly Hale, I innocently asked him, "What time of day is Vermeer depicting in his *View of Delft?*" Hale gave me a withering Brahmanical glance. "Vermeer time," he said.

Back to Wheelock. "There is virtually no narrative in a Vermeer," he said. "Each viewer must use his or her imagination." The *View of Delft,* painted circa 1660–1661, has only left the Mauritshuis twice— to go to London and Paris—and will probably never leave the Netherlands again. The painting has been extensively cleaned, and the public viewed the process through open glass at the Mauritshuis. During the cleaning of *Girl with a Pearl Earring,* two tiny white dots emerged at the corners of her mouth, brilliantly highlighting her expression. "I think I know that girl," I said. "So do I," Wheelock said. "But we are thinking of different people, both real!" It was time to see the show. "One other thing," he added, "is the enthusiasm of the guards. They, too, love the paintings. On one of those nightmare days when we didn't know if we would open, and then did open, a guard rushed up, held me in a viselike grip, and said, "We did it! We did it!"

In I went. The crowd was quiet, even reverential. Sure enough, a guard with longish hair came over and said, "Wouldn't it have been a shame to have closed *this?*" When I stand in front of art that has sur- vived three hundred or more years of human stupidity and brutality, yet retains a serene glow, a deeply visceral, stabilizing feeling comes over me. I was in heaven. For an embarrassingly long time, I stood in front of *The Little Street*. Each brick in the facades of the buildings has an intricate, sparkling life of its own. I could stare at the *View of Delft* forever. The dark reflections in the water and the yellowish light on the city behind, glistening, transcend what one normally thinks of as human achievement.

Dreams must end. Back to the Metroliner and the reality of Gotham. But, as the train left Union Station, there, on the right, under a lowering sky, and a patch of sunlight on a row of houses, I saw, for a glorious moment, an instance of Vermeer time.

Spring 1996